Hugo Grotius

Twayne's World Authors Series

Egbert Krispyn, Editor, The Netherlands

University of Georgia

TWAS 680

Ruit Hora HVGO GROTIVS, I.C. QVONDAM FISCI ADVOCATVS, ET REIP. ROTERODAMENSIS SYNDICVS. NATVS DELPHIS. ANNO CIƆIƆCLXXXIII

Depositum cæli, quod iure Batauia mater
  Horret, et haud credit se peperisse sibi
Talem oculis, talem ore tulit se maximus Hugo.
  Instar crede hominis, cætera crede Dei.

D. Heinsius 1614

Hugo Grotius

By Christian Gellinek

University of Florida

Twayne Publishers • *Boston*

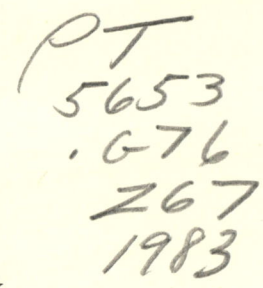

Hugo Grotius

Christian Gellinek

Copyright © 1983 by G.K. Hall & Company
All Rights Reserved
Published by Twayne Publishers
A Division of G. K. Hall & Company
70 Lincoln Street
Boston, Massachusetts 02111

Book Production by Marne B. Sultz

Book Design by Barbara Anderson

Printed on permanent/durable acid-free paper and bound in the United States of America.

Library of Congress Cataloging in Publication Data

Gellinek, Christian.
Hugo Grotius.

(Twayne's world author series; TWAS 680)
Bibliography: p. 147
Includes index.
1. Grotius, Hugo, 1583–1645—
Criticism and interpretation.
I. Title. II. Series.
PT5653.G76Z67 1982 878'.0409 82-12085
ISBN 0-8057-6525-5

Contents

About the Author
Preface
Acknowledgments
Chronology

> *Chapter One*
> Hugo Grotius's Life   1
>
> *Chapter Two*
> Poetical Works   6
>
> *Chapter Three*
> Philological Text Editions   44
>
> *Chapter Four*
> Scholarly Study of Patriotic History   65
>
> *Chapter Five*
> Legal Treatises   84
>
> *Chapter Six*
> Critical Evaluation   111

Notes and References   123
Selected Bibliography   147
Index   158

About the Author

Christian Gellinek is professor of Germanic Languages and Literature at the University of Florida in Gainesville. He was formerly a student of law at the University of Göttingen (Rudolf Smend), the Sorbonne (Levy-Brühl), Cape Town (Ben Beinert's History of Roman Law), a Latin instructor at Pickering College, Ontario, and an assistant/associate professor of German at Yale. He received his training at Göttingen (cand. jur.), Ontario College of Education (Latin, History), at Yale (Ph.D. 1964), and at Basel, Switzerland (Habilitation W.S. 1974–75), and was visiting professor at Basel, Poznań, Salt Lake City, and Münster. Gellinek has published monographs and essays on medieval German epics and chronicles, essays on aspects of Baroque Literature, as well as an introduction to linguistics. He is one of the coeditors of *Colloquia Germanica,* and was chairman of the Departments of German at Connecticut College and at the University of Florida.

He was appointed corresponding member of the journal *Grotiana,* issued at The Hague, in December 1981.

Preface

This study is the first comprehensive literary analysis ever undertaken of all the main works written in Latin and Dutch by Hugo Grotius. About a dozen biographies of value have been written during the last three hundred years, yet they focus on Grotius as father of international law, but not as the "considerable poet and dramatist."[1] For his poetic, dramatic, and historical work has generally remained unknown. So much so that even representative Dutch literary scholars sometimes fail to take notice where he deserves to be mentioned.[2] Next to oversight, there is bias to be found in Grotius scholarship. The leading seventeenth- and eighteenth-century biographers of Hugo Grotius, Caspar Brandt (1653–1696) and Adriaan van Cattenburgh (1664–1743), who cooperated in writing *Het Leven van H. de Groot*, were both Remonstrant-leaning theologians, hence perhaps too far on the defensive. Orthodox Calvinist or Lutheran writers, on the other hand, take a hostile attitude toward him. Most of Grotius's works were put on the Index of Forbidden Books by the Catholic Church of the seventeenth century, and sometimes not taken off until the twentieth. Joost van den Vondel, the greatest Dutch poet of the Netherlands' Golden Age, almost rhapsodically praises Grotius in several translations, poems, and as executor of Grotius's literary testament. By publishing his drama *Palamedes or Murdered Innocence* in 1625, the year of Prince Maurits's death, Vondel intimated to the literary public that Oldenbarnevelt (=Palamedes), and by implication Grotius, had been the victims of a "judicial murder."[3] The admiration of Grotius in France has had an uninterrupted tradition. J. de Burigny, who wrote an eighteenth-century biography of Grotius in French, was a theologically trained philosopher. In Germany, the conservative playwright August von Kotzebue published a flat four-act drama, *Hugo Grotius,* in 1803. Among Kotzebue's enemies was Dr. Heinrich Luden, professor of history at Jena and successor to Schiller, who gave a factual biographical reply in 1806. Unfortunately, his chapters take their romantic headings from Grotius's epitaph. In Britain, Grotius was known above all as the author of "True Religion." Charles Butler, who wrote on Grotius in

English in 1826, was a barrister. During the twentieth century the appreciation increased mainly in the Anglo-Saxon countries. Several judges and one barrister tried to come to grips with his legal works, Hamilton Vreeland (1917), W. S. M. Knight (1925) on several main works, van Eysinga, who published a short Dutch panegyric in 1945, and Edward Dumbauld, the last in a distinguished series, *The Life and Legal Writings of Hugo Grotius* (1969). In reading these and other studies by jurists focusing on the legal work by Grotius, one becomes well informed on one important aspect. Grotius, however, wore the robe only for eighteen years, but wielded the pen for fifty. Only a quarter of his publications deal with law and jurisprudence. Since these subjects stood at the center of attention for three hundred years, we purposely put them last in our treatment as his crowning achievement. They originated, however, in conjunction with Grotius's literary interests, and were substantially considered works of art by their author and his public. So this study undertakes to redress the imbalance insofar as his literary writing has been underrated. Our study, in other words, attempts to close a biographical gap from the point of view of a *literary* analysis. Our method pursued is structurally analytic and comparative. The order of presentation is by subject. We proceed chronologically under chapter headings insofar as that arrangement has proved possible. The titles are at first given in English renderings, whether English translations exist or not. Later on, Latin original titles or their standard abbreviations are used for the sake of convenience. The primary Latin titles are listed in the Selected Bibliography.

Christian Gellinek

University of Florida

Acknowledgments

This study contains my main work of the last five years at home and abroad, during which I had the fortune of working in the Peace Palace at The Hague and at Münster. The outcome here submitted integrates in a fashion the training received in various disciplines, least of all in theology. I wish to honor those teachers and ancient friends who managed to influence my thinking permanently: Herr Kreth, Latin and history, at Hamburg-Harburg, who talked of *De Jure Belli ac Pacis* in 1950; my revered Integrationist law teacher, the *Staats-* and *Kirchenrechtler* Prof. Rudolf Smend at Göttingen; my former *Remonstrantenpastor* at Friedrichstadt-on-Eider (Schleswig-Holstein), Dr. Adriaan van Peski, a well-known Dutch theologian; Prof. Emeritus F. S. C. Northrop at the Yale Law School. I started my first Grotius file in the Sterling Memorial Library in New Haven, Connecticut, in 1963, and came across the (Grotius) Publications of the Carnegie Endowment at Utah in 1977, when the project picked up momentum.

Particular thanks go to Dr. Charles F. Sidman, Dean of the College of Liberal Arts and Sciences at the University of Florida, for granting me a sabbatical leave, and the Fulbright Commission at Washington and Bonn for a Senior Research Fellowship, as well as the DAAD for a Summer Grant in 1980. Without the rather extensive support of the Librarians of the Peace Palace, Drs. J. B. van Hall and Drs. J. C. Schalekamp, and of the Universitätsbibliothek Münster, Dr. R. Reichelt, I could not have finished this project. Several Grotius scholars gave me valuable advice during interviews: in law, Prof. Dr. Robert Feenstra; in theology, Prof. Dr. G. H. M. Posthumus Meyjes, Professor Emeritus Dr. G. J. Hoenderdaal, Prof. Dr. E. J. Kuiper (all Leiden); in poetry, Dr. A. Eijffinger, Dra. Paula Witkam (both Grotius Instituut, Den Haag); and in history, Dr. Jan Den Tex. I am also obliged to Prof. Dr. Robert Walton (Münster) for advice on Reformed theology, and to Prof. Dr. W. Fikentscher (Munich) for his encouragement.

I wish to thank Dr. A. Eijffinger for having read proofs while on vacation: *"Ingens est vinculum, omnium honestarum literarum commune studium."*

Chronology

1583 Hugo Grotius born as Huigh de Groot at Delft, Holland, Netherlands.
1594 Grotius matriculates at the University of Leiden, Holland.
1597 Defense of philosophical theses.
1598 Is graduated Doctor of Laws at University of Orléans, France.
1599 Is admitted to the bar in Holland.
1601 Is supported as Latin historiographer of Holland.
1604 Becomes legal counsel to Prince Maurits van Nassau.
1607 Promoted to Attorney General and First Public Comptroller at three State Courts.
1608 Marriage to Marie van Reigersbergh.
1613 Ambassadorial mission to London. Promoted to City Governor of Rotterdam. Member of the States of Holland.
1617 Appointed to the Committee of the Counsellors. Pens the "Sharp Resolution" exacerbating a constitutional conflict between the States General and Holland.
1618 Maurits disbands the Militia of Utrecht, considered a threat to the Union. Johan van Oldenbarnevelt, the Land's Advocate, Grotius, and other officials arrested.
1619 Oldenbarnevelt executed. Grotius's prison term for life begins 5 June at the fortress Loevestein (confluence of Waal and Meuse).
1621 Celebrated escape from prison in a book chest, 22 March. Paris exile begins.
1625 Publishes his treatise on *Law of War and Peace*.

1631 Returns to Holland in defiance of outlaw status. Takes up law practice again. Is offered the Governor Generalship of the Dutch East Indies Company in Asia.

1632 In March, 2,000 guilders are put on his head. Is ordered to leave Holland on pain of rearrest. Leaves for Hamburg.

1634 Is called to Frankfurt-on-Main by the Swedish Chancellor, Count Axel Oxenstierna, offering him the Swedish ambassadorship to Paris at a yearly salary of 8,000 Riksdalers.

1635 Begins his diplomatic duties in Paris. Negotiates the Franco-Swedish Treaty of Compiègne, stipulating large subsidy payments to the Swedish campaign in Germany (Thirty Years War).

1641 The splitting of the peace negotiations in two German cities, which Grotius suggested as early as 1637, becomes Franco-Swedish policy. Opening of the peace negotiations at two Westphalian cities, Münster and Osnabrück, without Grotius's participation.

1644 Is relieved of his post in Paris 31 December.

1645 Decides to report back to Stockholm, where he declines alternative employment in the Swedish service. Travels hastily across the Baltic and is shipwrecked. Dies from exhaustion on 28 August en route in Rostock, Germany. His remains are brought home to Delft. Is buried in Delft on 3 October.

Chapter One
Hugo Grotius's Life

Huigh de Groot was born in Delft, Holland, on Easter Sunday, 10 April 1583. He was the oldest son of the mayor of Delft, Jan Huigh de Groot, M.A., LL.D. (1554–1640), and his lawful wife, Alida Borren van Overschie. His parents, although commoners, belonged to the ruling families of the land. Especially his father hailed from a distinguished line of Delft public officials. He was by profession a lawyer and a businessman exporting beer. De Groot was very talented. He composed lucid and pleasant Latin poetry, knew mathematics and astronomy well, and was a member of the Board of Regents at the University of Leiden from 1595 to 1617. His brother, Cornelis de Groot, a professor of law, presided over the faculty when Huigh enrolled. The University of Leiden, only twenty years old, was rapidly becoming Europe's most distinguished place of higher learning by 1600.

The de Groots leaned toward Calvinism. Mrs. de Groot was a practicing Catholic, however, until Huigh converted her to Calvinism. This conversion took place in 1595 and was significant for the twelve-year-old and his future roles. It is generally assumed that Huigh de Groot was baptized Calvinist, but no record in the registry of the Nieuwe Kerk in Delft exists today. For the first sixteen years Huigh liked to sign "Hugeianus" (= Huigh Jan) in honor of his father, whom he favored and tried to emulate. The adolescent underwent rapid intellectual growth and was proclaimed a prodigy early in his youth, so that his matriculation at the University of Leiden on 3 August 1594 was celebrated by its leading citizens. His father became a regent one year later. The son enrolled in the liberal arts program and majored in philosophy and classical philology, with a minor in Oriental languages. Soon the lad excelled in the art of critically reading and editing Latin and Greek texts, and published remarkable poetry in these languages in his freshman year.

The most outstanding university teacher at that time was Prof. J. J. Scaliger, a French-Italian Huguenot, who considered Hugo Grotius and his friend Daniel Heinsius (1580–1655) his most talented disciples. In 1597 Hugo defended his non–degree-earning philosophical theses, and if he studied the subject of law at Leiden, he must have done so in his spare time. First he befriended the Calvinist theologian and court preacher Dr. Johannes Uitenbogaert at The Hague, the seat of the government. Second, the Land's Advocate, a de-facto prime minister of the United Netherlands, Johan van Oldenbarnevelt (1547–1619), took him under his political tutelage. Shortly after the Tolerance Edict of Nantes was promulgated, guaranteeing a degree of equality of rights between the two major Christian confessions, the Dutch delegation attached young Grotius to its ranks on a mission to the French Court. After a convincing professional defense in Roman law Hugo was presented an honorary doctor of laws degree at the University of Orléans. On this occasion King Henry IV congratulated him and handed him a golden medallion with the king's portrait weighing as heavily on the shoulders of the honoree as the king's quip: "Voilà le miracle de Hollande." This scene, his receving the chain with the portrait of the king who had converted to Catholicism because "Paris was worth a mass," stayed with Hugo throughout his life. It was immortalized by the famous Delft engraver Jacques de Gheyn. The publisher of Hugo's first book, a philological text edition on the liberal arts, Chr. Raphelengius, decided to attach the engraving as a frontispiece to the edition. Grotius looks odd and childlike on the print.[1]

In 1599 he was admitted to the bar, the highest there was, namely before the Court and High Council of Holland. Not quite two years later he acquired another office, and was appointed Latin historiographer of Holland in 1604. In between these years he penned his most outstanding Latin poetry, his first drama, and his germinal States Parallels in draft form. He also refereed and wrote on freedom of navigation and intercontinental trade with the support of the Dutch East Indies Company. Upon the recommendation of Prince Maurits he was appointed attorney general and first public comptroller, a kind of fiscal advocate with prosecuting powers, at the Courts of Holland, Westfriesland, and Zeeland. This was no less than the highest legal office a lawyer could hold. Thus at age twenty-four and at a yearly salary of 1,000 guilders, he retired as barrister after seven years of brilliant service.

His father arranged an appropriate marriage with the daughter of the mayor of Veere (Zeeland), Marie van Reigersbergh (1590–1653), an exceptionally able and courageous woman, with whom he had eight children, five of whom reached adulthood. He was twenty-five and famous, she was eighteen, the right kind of woman, and much in love with her *allerliefste*. In June 1613, after a short diplomatic mission to London, he was rewarded with the city governorship of Rotterdam, as successor to Elias Oldenbarnevelt, who in turn had followed his older brother, now the chief policymaker in the United Provinces. Hugo's salary was doubled to 2,000 guilders a year. Before he undertook the move to Rotterdam, he negotiated the granting of tenure by the city, which would not be honored in the end. Grotius climbed higher and higher on the political ladder, and was considered with some envy the eventual successor to Oldenbarnevelt. As governor he became a political civil servant, a member of parliament, and finally, in 1617, an influential but controversial member of the Committee of Maurits's Counsellors.

As leader of the Remonstrants' party he was unable to avert the Council's recommendation to convene a Remonstrant-hostile Church Synod at Dordrecht. In 1618, the commanding general of the Dutch army, Maurits, disbanded the militia of Utrecht, a military outfit which, on orders of Grotius, challenged his chief military authority, and hence threatened the constitutional integrity of the Union. Grotius had penned a sharply worded resolution, challenging the constitutionality of the prince's proposed measures, and also held a conception of Holland's dutifulness in Church governance, which did not appeal to Maurits, for it did not represent the feeling of the majority of Dutchmen. Maurits was obliged by oath to uphold the prevalent Calvinist religious belief system of Holland. After long hesitation he reacted to the crisis in the manner of a soldier and used a special weapon. He had his closest public servants, the aging Oldenbarnevelt and his right-hand man, Grotius, arrested on unspecific charges and thrown into the central Hague prison at the *Binnenhof*. It must suffice here to allude merely to the outcome of the political lawsuit, during which a special court consisting of lawyers, considered biased to the accused, passed the verdict of guilty. Barnevelt, the architect of Dutch independence, was publicly beheaded in his seventy-first year. Hugo Grotius, half his age, was condemned to life imprisonment. The former had refused outright to ask for clemency; the latter refused to ask formally. Once jailed at

Loevestein the ex–attorney general started to write even more intensively than he had before. After twenty-one months he fled in disguise, leaving his crafty wife substituting for him in the cell, and arrived safely via Antwerp in Paris, where Louis XIII granted him safety and indemnity. Since the famous refugee refused to convert to Catholicism, his political value was diminished, and he was offered no position either at the court or at the university. Thus he had to live as an exile, meagerly supported by a pension promised by the monarch, the payments of which Cardinal Richelieu deliberately delayed. Grotius did not receive royalties for his books, and hence must have been supported by his Dutch relatives, for his own estate had been confiscated.

His fortunes turned only after the Protestant Swedish Chancellor, who worked within an unholy alliance with the Cardinal, tried to press subsidy payments out of the French treasury. The most unlikely candidate, the internationally renowned scholar Grotius, was chosen as emissary to Paris. He had three rare qualities to commend him for the delicate mission: he was thought to be impartial toward either major Christian religion, as he belonged to the third one, moderate Calvinism; second, he was principled, and hence possessed the stamina to deal with Cardinal Richelieu and his wily Père Joseph; third, he was known to be utterly unbribable. Historians have traditionally underestimated Grotius's ten years of Swedish diplomatic service in Paris. Thanks to Grotius's dogged skill and mastery in gathering intelligence, the promised subsidy payments to Sweden, although coming forth painfully slowly, never totally ceased, and therefore permanently turned the fortune of the Protestants and the enemies of the German Empire. Oxenstierna used a principled Dutch scholar-diplomat on the slippery ground of Paris, and his Swedish wheeler-dealer, Dr. Johann Adler Salvius, on the stately parquet of the Free Hanseatic city of Hamburg, where the two had met between 1632–34. When the German Emperor proposed the Preliminary Peace of Prague in 1635, he still held the upper hand in the Thirty Years War. Ten years later, after tough negotiations in Hamburg and Paris, carefully coordinated by Oxenstierna, Salvius, and Grotius, Ferdinand's dominance over this Empire from within Germany had passed to the foreign crowns of France and Sweden. The beneficiaries were not only the two victorious countries, but also principally the Netherlands, whom Grotius thus indirectly served more formidably than the forgotten Dutch chargé d'affaires in Paris.

Hugo Grotius's Life

To his deep disappointment Grotius was not asked to represent Sweden or any country as delegate or as mediator when the peace negotiations began at Münster and Osnabrück, Westphalia, in 1644. He hurriedly wrote letters to influence proceedings slipping from his grip. New political regimes were trying to assert themselves both in France and in Sweden. Grotius was known to both sides not to be the type to deal in reparations, satisfactions, and shady bargains. His new sovereign, Queen Christina of Sweden, having come of age recently, gave him notice toward the end of 1644. Since his contract again stipulated tenure, she offered him, during his visit to Stockholm, alternative employment.[2] He declined, and instead of awaiting the official ship he hastily retreated across the Baltic Sea. His boat was caught in a storm and shipwrecked before the Bay of Dantzig. He died from exhaustion en route on an unexplained diplomatic mission to Münster.

Grotius found his resting place at the Nieuwe Kerk, Delft. He is buried among members of the Dutch Royal family, only a few steps away from Maurits van Nassau. Traditionally, only royalty is laid to rest in that church. Hugo Grotius is the only commoner honored by an epitaph in an exceptional fashion. In 1648 when peace was concluded at Münster and Osnabrück, the supplemental judgment of 1620 which condemned him ex post facto as as a traitor, which he and Oldenbarnevelt were not, was finally nullified. His faithful widow, who had been dismissed from Loevestein shortly after her husband's escape and had stayed with him in Paris almost constantly, had pressed on with her charges to have Grotius exonerated.

Today, by common agreement, the jurist, scholar, statesman, theologian, writer, and world diplomat Hugo Grotius is considered to have been the most renowned man of letters and learning seventeenth-century Netherlands brought forth. The seminal topics of his works are still alive today.

Chapter Two
Poetical Works
Neo-Latin Drama

Adam in Exile. In the year 1600, when Giordano Bruno was burned alive at the stake for professing his conviction that the earth turned around the sun, the seventeen-year-old lawyer Grotius conceived of a bold literary project: he was going to write a drama that was supposed to be "delightful by itself." He was going to excel in a literary genre in which "his generation was less productive." The finished play "could not displease any Christian." In other words he wanted to dramatize "the very first story of Holy Scripture," the account of man's fall from paradise as narrated in Genesis 3, as he relates in the dedication to his first drama, *Adamus Exul,* from which we quoted.

This tragedy was published in The Hague in August 1601. On the occasion of its publication, his friend and contributor Daniel Heinsius topped the compliment that Joseph Justus Scaliger (1540–1609), their teacher at the University of Leiden, had just paid Hugo. Scaliger had written that Grotius was a precocious boy-philosopher. Heinsius now dubbed his friend a person who had been born a mature man *(Grotius vir natus est).* Heinsius only expressed the high esteem in which a whole generation of Leiden humanists held their fellow alumnus, and their poems, among them that of Heinsius, were appended to Grotius's book.

Today *Adamus Exul* is almost completely forgotten. Leiden and its humanism of the past, as far as the American student of literature is concerned, have fallen into oblivion. A member of the Grotius Institute at The Hague recently claimed that *Adam in Exile* lacked a clear dramatic unity.[1] It is true that a structural analysis of this sacred drama cannot be found anywhere in the vast secondary literature on Grotius's works, but the young poet explicitly indicates to his "fair critic" (v. 62–63) in his dedication that his tragedy has a framework.

The technique employed he describes as deliberately "anachronistic" (*per anticipationem*, 65–66). His play *(scæna)* displays its dramatic persons on a reduced scale, as "interlocutors" who are not bound by time that passes during the action. The place of the play is defined as the Garden of Eden. The persons do not represent fully developed characters, and yet they do have character, as we shall notice.

With one notable exception, the interlocutors are arranged in opposite pairs. Satan operates first in human shape, later on as a reptile in disguise. The heavenly voices speak individually as angels, or collectively as paradisiacal chorus. Adam is paired with Eve; and there are two special trees planted in the Garden, the permitted tree of life, and the forbidden tree of knowledge, of which the latter is identified by its fair bark (1000). Since God is all powerful, His voice stays unpaired or unique. It appears only toward the end of the fifth and last act.

Satan, the chorus, and Adam each appear in all by one act, Eve in all but Acts I and II, and the angel once in act III. All interlocutors are to be considered ageless because they operate before postparadisiacal time. Each act gives prominence to one speaker only: Act I to the plotting Satan, Act II to the angel praising God and His creation, Act III to steadfast Adam, Act IV to yielding woman. Technically, she is given her traditional name only at the end of Act V, which tells of God driving the couple out of Eden. The two principal dramatic antagonists are "good," represented by heavenly voices, and "evil" (falling good), represented by the creatures (the tempter and the tempted ones).

The two sides speak to each other in different meters. Significantly and indicative of the working of fate, both Satan (the fallen angel) and Eve/Adam (the doomed human) speak in the same rhythmic language throughout the drama, namely iambic trimeters: e.g., Satan: *Et ámpla vácuó spatiá laxántur lóco* (111) ("And undefinable space grows more infinite in Paradise") or Adam: *Méa cúlpa nón est. Crímen hújus féminae est* (1866) ("I plead not guilty—my wife committed the crime").[2] This meter is also used by the faithful angel of Act II. Grotius must have implied by his choice that this meter is appropriate for the chosen ones, even if they happen to fall afterwards. The chorus, on the other hand, speaks in all principal lyrical meters, iambic (υ–́), trochaic (–́υ), dactylic (–́υυ), or anapaestic (υυ–́), eleven syllables prevailing to a line. The praise of the Lord and of his paradise calls for the greatest metric variety possible. We are not surprised that the meter employed by God's voice is unique to Him. It is the trochaic tetrameter: e.g., Voice: *Adáme, quás nunc te ín látebrás prorípis?* (1839) ("O, Adam, into what lurkingplace are you hurriedly trying to escape?") This meter is the one preferred by the Roman dramatist Seneca (5 B.C.–A.D. 65) and by Christian hymn writers.

The action in *Adam in Exile* consists of pleas presented by the two opposing forces of good and evil, between which man is torn. Time can still "curb itself" (843–844), as if it consisted of celestial or satanic vibrations. But the switch from before to after the fall is clearly marked by a metric change from ∪$\stackrel{\_}{}$ to $\stackrel{\_}{}$∪, from the innocently flowing iambic to the harshly commanding trochaic. Whereas the eating of the apple took but a second in Act IV, the expulsion at the end of Act V will last to doomsday, not discussed in this drama.

We may therefore state in our first summarization that de Groot, who includes himself among the ranks of poets (v. 66, dedication), tries to convey metaphorically (*in comparationibus*, 64–65) his vision of original sin: he chooses metrically ordered images as his medium. We would have to label *Adamus Exul* a voice drama, a tragedy to be recited in solemn fashion like a mystery or morality play, if acted out physically.[3] We would prefer to call it a martyr drama, since the expulsion begins the original human suffering. In stating this, we have by no means exhausted our analysis. Is it just another version of the many martyr plays of the "celestial" type? We think there are dramatic, juridical, and perhaps also theological aspects to the play that have not been properly discussed with respect to Grotius's subsequent thinking. Some of these aspects are listed in the author's own index appended to the original edition of 1601.[4] First of all, let us consider the dramatic aspect. It would be puzzling to the reader of Grotius's play if we considered it a somewhat distant forerunner of epic theater. Now the Christian reader of *Adam in Exile* is invited to ponder seriously the forbidden rape of knowledge. He is supposed to ask himself how *he* would have resisted the brainwashing of the sideward-moving serpent (*tramite obliquo*, 1034), how *he* would have exerted his free will, and finally, how *he* will face his own (predestined?) death in this state of sin. The dramatic climax of the play is, in our opinion, not man's reach toward the tree of knowledge, but rather the first couple's resolve to face up to God's severe punishment, their expulsion, as it were, from their intended homeland.

Eden was created as a place for man to live. After the first human generation wanted to be like God, their hold over paradise is withdrawn. The devil knew the nefarious character of their crime (16) beforehand. From his point of view the stern Lord's exerted authority was "harsh and tyrannical" (79; 1663). In the diabolical analysis paradise should be destroyed, as it actually is burned at God's command in Act V. Satan, the former Lucifer, is a fallen inhabitant. His opening soliloquy, Act I, 1–232, and his closing address in Act V, 1530–1588, are spoken out of envy in the vein of a pagan warrior crying for his rival's banishment. In advance, he is gloating over man's (and hence mankind's) defeat. His tone, as has been noted, is reminiscent of Seneca's dramas *Hercules' Fury,* 1–124, and *Hercules' Oetaeus,* 240 ff.[5]: e.g., "Do I forget myself, or *does* the whole earth truly tremble under my own weight?" (14–15). Here rages not only a vile temper but an equally proud former peer of the kingdom. Grotius seems to have grafted the Greek myth of raging fury onto the Jewish myth of falling virtue. This combination of separate myths helps to parallelize the states of mind expressed by Satan and by his opponent Adam. What happened to Satan is going to happen to Adam also, is his prediction. God expelled the former Lucifer in such a fashion that Satan could not commit suicide. Adam faces a comparable dilemma in vv. 1677–1778 and in 1815. Adam's choice is interpreted by Satan as a "form of slavery" (*mancipia,* 100). He is trying to achieve Adam and Eve's subsequent fall, in order to gain triumphant satisfaction (1537; 124–30; 937).

The characterization of God as "thundering" (e.g., 930) gives Grotius's associations away: God was to be seen as associated with thundering Jove (*Jupiter tonans*); and Satan was upgraded by an association with Jove's brother Pluto.[6] This plutonized Satan adorns his speech with military metaphors: e.g., "to fight perpetual wars" (130; 135; 937), the "enemy" (126; 149; 842; 948). Man's expected punishment will surpass his own, and result in expulsion from paradise. Satan anticipates that the creation will yield to initial chaos again (1560). Rebellion is part of his nature throughout the drama. In this respect

Adam and Eve are to catch up with Satan. We can deduce that the battle between good and evil is presented as a palace rebellion against the commands in terms of civil war (295; 878; 1021).

Satan's first offer to Adam consists of a peace treaty (877; 941).[7] Since Adam refuses, Satan demands: "Stop the war!" (910–11). Although their pact is supposed to rest on "good faith" (863), feigned by Satan, it actually consists of perfidy in disguise. Adam is told that as Satan's peer he would share equal power. Recognizing the tempter for what he is, Adam vehemently refuses. The prospective viceroy Adam refuses to enter an alliance for legal reasons: "I am God's client!" (931); "I am pledged to Him by mutual trust and good faith" (930); "content in my position I seek no further alliance" (933). Adam, God's stoic subruler, fears his Lord. He will, in other words, not take part in such a conspiracy (942). Throughout Act III (and elsewhere) we come across pleas and arguments betraying Grotius's professional experience as a trial lawyer.

It was Adam who accidentally met Satan at the beginning of Act III, and it is now the serpent who crawls toward Eve at the opening of Act IV. Eve, for whom "sister to Adam" is used in v. 1766, seems to take on the role of Pluto's twin sister, Glauca. Thus exalted she addresses the serpent first (although she never saw this animal before). Arguments ensue which consume more than twice the length of words exchanged between Adam and Satan (842–967 vs. 1034–1327). This exchange is subtler than the verbal bout between man and serpent. This is remarkable, since Adam knew his enemy beforehand, otherwise he could not have addressed him as "rebel against God" on sight (878). Nevertheless, Eve is not at a forensic disadvantage. Satan asks her whether the ruler's governance is such that He gave her dominance over the whole earth, but will not let her enjoy the control of the whole garden of Eden. Slyly creation is reinterpreted as a process with fixed and fatal consequence (1080; 1074), including eventual yielding to temptation anyhow. "Your death does not depend on the appetite for one apple from the tree of knowledge" (1081 ff.). Even punishment (the death penalty promised by God in Genesis 2:17) is part of nature, muses a suddenly fatalistic advocate, as is death (1094). God would not have created such fruit had He meant it to ripen in vain (1104). Subtly, the discussion about an absolute command given by God (762–63) is shifted to the possible reasons for His commands.

Eve's mind is still dutifully doubtful about the sense of the law applicable here (1111). Satan supplied her with God's hidden side of his command. As if He were Saturnus (the father of the twins Pluto and Glauca) He is suspected by Satan of harboring a feeling of envy toward anyone who would like to taste the goodness hidden in these special apples (1129). Hence this special restriction amounts to "servitude" (1132; 1137). Finally, Eve comes around to wanting to know about the hidden motivation for goodness (1169–70). Satan then describes the beauty of independent moral reasoning to her, claiming that the consumption of the fruit would make her, the eater, no less than a goddess (1217; 1394). When weighing the eating in her mind, she is not thinking of her mate at all. Suddenly, she realizes that plucking the apple would sensually please her (1264; 1173); she bursts out: "The future of mankind depends on this single bite!" (1287). Technically her crime is committed by *foresight* (1299). The perpetration proceeds in three stages: "I touched the tree!" "I plucked the apple!" She feels accused before she goes through the final stage of eating. Her awareness is in keeping with the poet's proleptic style of anticipation (65–66 of the dedication), which we discussed at the beginning of this chapter. She anticipates that she will be condemned for spiritual high treason, termed *lèse majesté* (1306).[8] Thus Eve stands condemned in advance even by herself.

As the Devil sarcastically remarks, Adam returns late for dinner (1327). And this slow return (1328) proves perilous. Adam comes back too early for Eve's developing any sense of remorse. Stubbornly she asks him not to prejudge the case against her (1367). She defends her rebellion until her husband experiences an emotional breakdown. Suddenly he is outraged, as if the furies were driving him mad (Act IV, 1350 ff.). Let us focus on their principal arguments with respect to their behavior toward God. Eve would rather be promoted to a goddess than continue as "a toiling human being" (1374; 1394). Adam reprimands her that she could become innocent by true contrition of heart. In view of the existing matrimonial bond she proposes an alliance between them. Her aim is to achieve "felicity" reminiscent of the Devil's formerly proposed "felicity of mind" (1173). Grotius seems to have coined the famous phrase "You have nothing to fear but fear itself" (Eva: *hoc timere ipsum time,* 1426). Adam succeeds in steadying himself: first he regains his faith toward his Lord, and second, toward his mate. But his loyalties are in conflict with one another. He realizes that his love toward his God (*aeterna fide,* 1429; 1442–43) should come first; on the other hand, he has to determine whether he should reject his wife or join her in the crime. To him, conjugal should rank above filial love. He rationalizes that God's commands show a hierarchical order, some taking precedence over others; thus he is given an ethical choice.[9] By an error of reasoning Adam concludes that it *is* God's will (1460) that he should eat from the tree. He thinks that the loss of *one* apple is a minor detail[10] compared to fulfilling conjugal duty.[11] He experiences no sensual pleasure such as Eve had. Immediately after consumption Adam pales and falls sick (1465). The chorus, in a mixture of semibiblical and Senecaesque terminology,[12] anticipates and mourns the impending castastrophe that is to befall mankind.

In the opening scene of Act V Satan exults in a double personal triumph. First, Eve's prospective descendants will be born, burdened with sin, as if they had been sired by him—*liberos gignes mihi* (1552).[13] Second, he anticipates that Eve and her progeny will return creation back to "ancient chaos" (1560). Satan also relishes Adam's madness. Eve gradually nurses her husband back to semisanity (1612; 1618). But he does not listen attentively to reason as yet. Instead he offers God his head in exchange for his crime, indicating capital punishment. His is a very moving speech in the original (1652–77). It culminates in his death wish: "I can, I must, I want to die!" (1677). The first of men—and already "a living cadaver" thinking only of suicide. Eve: "Don't aggravate your despair by piling crime upon crime" (1699–1702). "It is up to the arbiter of life to lift your yoke!" (1707). Unconvinced he avows: "I believed you once too often!" (1730). Only Eve's final appeal to Adam's valor as a male (1749) changes his mind, set on suicide. Noticing her "splendid virtue" (1753) he wants to expiate their "common guilt" by his suicide (1761–62; 1795). Her rebuttal: "Don't you widow me!" "Kill me too!" "If you don't know how, I'll instruct you!" (1779–82). And "I won't live without you, but you can die together with me!" (1808). At this point Adam awakes from his demented state and goes along with her wish. Thus he makes himself Satan's companion of fate, intensely experiencing the pain of not being able to perish (1815). The culprit's leafy hair stands up like the garden's foliage.

Summoned by his judge, Adam shifts the blame for his crime (1427; 1663) to his mate (1866). Eve, who yielded to temptation by deceptive reasoning, pleads reduced capacity because of her sex (1873). Satan is adjudged the mastermind of the crime (*minister sceleris*, 1877). For the deception part, he is condemned to eternal hunger pangs; but as fallen angel he is not punishable for man's "homicide" (1894) or aberration from the predestined course.[14] The judge then determines their various degrees of participation in his conspiracy against Him. The prediction by Satan that evil will completely triumph over the fate of the human soul (1550) does not come true. God will irreversibly, but not eternally, enslave man to evil. The paradisiacal light having shone in their hearts before the fall will be rekindled by their potential salvation (1903–4). Eve will get a chance to prove herself by the eternal wars she will have to fight against evil (1913; 937). God's promise of eventually sending Christ—here referred to as "Himself" (1914)—will make this predicted warfare rewarding in the end. Eve, and future women with her, are condemned to suffering labor pains and to taking second place to man, in keeping with her own choice of v. 1810: *viventem sequor* (see above). Adam's punishment is less harsh (1939 ff.) as he was only an accomplice (1942).

God changes the whole earth into a sterile, dry, and exhausted place (1945). Man is, like Sisyphus, condemned to toiling on that unyielding soil forever. Since Adam and Eve escaped detention in the underworld, their sentence is considered clement (1959). They are, however, condemned to hard labor in a symbolic sense also. In the case of Eve the penalty is directed toward herself and her reproduction. In the case of Adam the sentence challenges his mettle as mankind's gardener, having to make barren earth produce. Their sentence is final. No appeal is entertained. Only the arrival of the Savior in the far distant future will overcome the banishment from paradise.

In symbolic fashion the two trees once representing life (reproduction) and knowledge (potential deification) burn to ashes. Man-in-effigy is consumed by "fire without flames" (2008–9). This celestial fire spreads its heat and thereby drives out the couple. The cathartic fire, unmoved by their farewell cries, betokens that the Lord of their paradise lost does not forgive them.

So far in our analysis we have treated the basic dramatic aspects of Grotius's first play. We have come across several legal problems. The crimes in chronological order of their occurrence are deception amounting to fraud, breach of promise, theft, "homicide," instigation to theft; and their punishments amounted to perpetual hunger, renewed exile, perpetual pain and toil in exile. We found out that the misdeed turned out to become the crime par excellence, as both Satan and Eve had predicted it would in the first place.[15]

This problem leads us to the difficult question of what precisely is a (sacred) martyr drama that rather faithfully paraphrases the biblical text and yet completely changes its ethical thrust? Maybe the voice of the angel could aid in clarifying this essential point. He states at the beginning of *Adamus Exul* that the human couple is equipped with the use of speech (*usus rationis,* 335).[16] They can unimpededly communicate with the devil. But can they have developed a moral faculty? That seems doubtful to this critic. All the couple knows from the beginning is that eating from that particular tree is forbidden (690–91). The consequence for trespassing this particular command is death (1865). God's warning that He would implement this punishment is not heeded. God can neither renege on His given word, for that would be contrary to his own nature,[17] nor can he expand upon his set of rules, except by adding clemency. He could, for instance, take on human form (1914) and *Himself* act as Savior of mankind (1916) and thus become the hope of salvation (1962).

This very connection between Godhead and Himself *(Deus et Ipse),* a promised re-creation of His own selfhood, expands the original convenant between God and man. Apparently, Grotius's god did not really hand a large enough authority *(imperium)* over to man so that he would have sufficient self-dominance before the Fall takes place, but only afterward.[18] He makes up for this deficit, extending his paternal power *(patria potestas)* in Himself, by promising to create a God-Man (Jesus) out of Himself and mortal woman whose son will have to suffer the predestined and promised death on behalf of mankind at the cross.[19]

Since mercy expressed in a drama (even one of such dimensions as *Adam in Exile*) lessens the dramatic effect, we consider the term "martyr drama" applicable to *Adamus Exul*. We do not, however, define it as a passion play, since (despite its rich Senecaesque overlay) Grotius, by interlacing Christ's promised arrival, enhances the essence of the Old Testament drama. In this changed light, Christ's coming is taking on the character of a *deus ex machina*. That is why the more mature Grotius wished in hindsight he had never published *Adam in Exile,* and excluded it from his own sacred poetry.[20] *Adamus Exul* humanizes original sin by building an imaginative bridge over the abyss. This early drama of man's martyrdom succeeds by typologically grafting the Christian gospel onto Genesis. The drama *Adam in Exile* is carried toward its conclusion by releasing humanistic sparks of hope, which are meant to embellish the rigor surrounding Genesis's first human narrative.

Christ's Passion. By the time Hugo Grotius published his second tragedy, *Christus Patiens,* in April 1608, he was the author of some twenty thousand Latin verses[21] and internationally famous. He was certainly fully accepted as a member of the illustrious circle of Leiden humanists. Before his impending marriage to Marie van Reigersbergh he closed the phase of his "youthful religious poetry." At least so it appeared to him in hindsight when he wrote to his friend Gerard J. Vossius (1577–1649): "By writing Christ's Passion I had taken up again my ancient audacity, begun, as if by puerile impulse, in my first drama, Adam in Exile."[22]

Although the title *Christus Patiens,* suggested to Grotius by his teacher Joseph Justus Scaliger, literally means "suffering savior," the modern reader should not be misled into assuming that he confronts a passion play.[23] For the author superimposed "tragedy" as title over the subtitle "Christus Patiens." Second, Grotius specifically stated in his foreword no less than five times that he was trying to rework this theme, "undoubtedly a centerpiece of our religion," into a tragic play (lines 24–26/7). The tragedy is meant to be read as a book drama and presupposes more than a mere familiarity with the New Testament. It addresses itself to readers who appreciate "poetical exercises," although it "offers only a small margin to poetical invention." Furthermore, Grotius felt that the Passion was "the most dignified story for [the genre of] a tragedy." He does not intend "to change the biblical event" or "to open religious piousness to doubt."

It is understandable that no critic we know of, has so far produced a description of the drama's inherent structure. Even the most recent introduction to the modern critical edition by A. Eijffinger[24] does not offer such an analysis. But time has come to present such a study. Given Grotius's penetrating analytical powers of mind, it would be astonishing if one could not distill his second play's structure from a close reading of the text.

In view of the dual nature of Jesus' trial and condemnation, the plot takes on a judicial character. For this lawsuit is both predestined to unfold, exemplarily leading to *our* condemnation, and political in kind, possibly leading to *His* acquittal. As such, the trial fulfills Judeo-Christian predictions. Since, however, it had to be conducted in a biased human court, it must proceed outside the bounds of Roman and Jewish law. Certainly, the lawyer Hugo Grotius was fully aware of this predicament. In fact, he created his own vision out of this legal and at the same time (supralegal) spiritual tension. Precisely this tension suggested the poetic structure of his play to Grotius. During Jesus' betrayal, interrogation, torture, conviction, and crucifixion, there exists a sacrificial tension between fate, as willed by God the Father, and misfortune, as bequeathed by God to his son. By introducing a sacrificial element into the condemnation, the secular and political aspects of the trial are intensified. Pilate fulfills God's will unknowingly. Grotius probably shared Sir Philip Sidney's (1554–1586) belief that politics was God's art, not man's.[25] God used an otherwise obscure Roman procurator, Pontius Pilate, to carry out His divine plan of saving mankind. Pilate dissociates himself from the tenor of his pronouncement by washing his hands of guilt. He condones the execution because of his fear that a future rebellion will endanger his position at the emperor's court in Rome. So the drama's centerpiece (*caput*) is clearly Act III, legally, symmetrically, and hence dramatically. This pivotal act is framed by Act II (backward looking) and by Act IV (forward looking), as if it were the center of a triptych. Act II focuses on Caiphas, as if he were an attorney general of the accusatory Jewish crowd (*turba Judaeorum*) rather than a high priest. In Act IV, on the other hand, Christ's suffering on the cross—which taste and dramatic rules forbid to produce on stage directly—is narrated by two messengers. The three center acts (II–III–IV) are framed by Act I (backward looking), spoken in the form of a prologue by Jesus (and a chorus of Jewish Women) during which he both anticipates and accepts mankind's punishment, and by Act V (anagnoritically forward and backward looking) in which the senators Joseph of Arimathea and Nicodemus apocryphally settle Christ's burial. The epilogue marks the beginning of a new Christian era, where John, adopted by Mary at Jesus' command, helps her overcome the lifelong grief for her son by spiritual compassion *(pietà)*. He thus triggers the recognition of her role as "God's mother" (*anagnorisis,* i.e., reversing recognition). Act I centers around Jesus' speaking (but not praying) alone to God, Act II around Caiphas as high priest and the chorus of Jews, and Act III around Pilate as judge, representing the Emperor of Rome as procurator. Act IV puts the cross as the symbol of Christ's martyrdom into the center (without showing it visibly on stage), and Act V finally brings the catharsis into the aggrieved heart of Jesus' mother by John's spiritual intercession. The pattern of the five-act structure is thus spiritually symmetrical.

Grotius exerts descriptive discretion. Actual death and resurrection are not shown. In Act I God stays unseen; in Act II the door of the interrogation scene stays unopened; in Act III Jesus' possible defense remains unstated; in Act IV the crucifixion is blocked out; and in Act V Christ's burial is not depicted. Acts III and IV are parallel in that they harbor monologues. Acts II and V, however, show dialogue structure by the nonchorus speeches. The first scenes of Acts II and III are paralleled, too: there, Peter the coward condemns himself; here, Judas, the betrayer of the Lord, demands reacceptance of the blood money; the second scenes of Acts II and III also have parallel structures: Caiphas betrays the Jews in front of Pilate, just as Judas betrays himself in front of Caiphas. The two court sessions (Act II Pilate/Caiphas; Act III Pilate/the Jewish people) proceed along parallel lines, as if the person takes the preceding person's place or function. This "swelling" technique seems to betray traces of the Baroque fugue structure, employed in chamber music. The place of the play lies between Jerusalem and Golgotha; the time from White Thursday to Good Friday encompasses less than twenty-four hours, entirely in keeping with the prescribed biblical setting. Since the group of participating persons is small, the rules pertaining to the three units of classical drama (as few persons as possible, one place and uninterrupted time) are clearly satisfied. It is the formal side of the "non-continuous action"[26] which is problematical. Since the play does not present an orderly secular lawsuit, conducted according to a penal code, it stays mysteriously obscure. The figures participating in the mystery are the biblical ones familiar to the reader. They are party to a sentence which was planned and accepted beforehand since the beginning of time (v. 4) as part of God's will, unknown to Pilate. The poet makes his Jesus figure particularly concerned with the question: when does the time come? (6; 74–75). This manneristic concern with rushing to a predestined conclusion introduces a dramatic tempo which wants to outpace the clock. It is driven by human fear of the impending passion.

The 300-odd lines spoken by the choruses are set apart. The interlocutors use an asclepiadean (= trochaic) meter to orchestrate and help release the spiritual tension built up by this passion: e.g., 1126 *Quáe natúra tuí / póena plácet tibí?* ("Which punishment, Nature, will please you?"). Beside the asclepiadean transgressions, the rich metric variety of *Adamus Exul* is gone, with iambic trimeter prevailing throughout the *Christus Patiens:* e.g., *Mens ánte córpus péndet: Hórrescó nefás* (90). Chorus and figures recite rather sententiously (in imitation of Seneca). His tendency toward imitating a classical dramatist is such an outstanding feature of both of Grotius's dramas that one can perceive in the figure of Jesus a christianized Hercules, and in his mother, Mary, Hercules' mother, Alcmene.[27] Grotius deliberately entwines the biblical scenarium with antique dramatic myth in order to heighten the effect of the Passion. The basis for this technique of fusing biblical and classical sources is the belief that drawing such parallels would ennoble and doubly verify the plot. Even pagan sources are used in aid of attesting to the greatness of Christianity in whichever form and shape. Classical parallels, in Grotius's and other contemporary writers' works, increase the veracity of the Christian message.[28] In the Latin monologues, dialogues, and choruses of these five acts, spoken in classical meter, one perceives not only traces of a christianized Seneca, but, more important, one meets a senecized Christ. The sophisticated public of the early seventeenth century must have preferred to hear of the manneristically fused traditions over and above the historically separate ones.

Let us return now to the question of the dramatic timing. In our opinion, the tension between biblical passion time (less than a day and a night) and dramatic time (narrated in all its gruesome details) creates the room in which the play exists on its merits or fails to convince. Insofar as these two time axes are coordinated, spherical time grinds to a halt: the sun stands still, the earth trembles in a quake, the temple crashes, the purple rain falls, etc. Time, as it were, is bent into halting original sin by a sacrifice guaranteeing an antidoom to mankind. Since God's preordained act is accepted by his prime sufferer and martyr who is a "born exile" (11), the time during execution is also quickening its pace; it is, to use the poet's words, "racing toward its fulfillment" (74–75).[29] This deadly fate is one of fulfillment for the living, not one of deserved punishment for the sufferer. Jesus realizes this paradox in vv. 82–83. He even anticipates the onset of crucifixion time by confessing: "My mind hangs on the cross before my body. I shudder at the crime" (90). The scenario cannot be stopped anymore since it was set at the time of the fall of mankind (101). "But God's eternal law *and* predestined order of future events forbid a change of events" (99–100).[30] And: "I perish so that the orbit of the world will not wither!" Even: "I take upon myself the punishments of all the worlds" (118–19). Christ talks here as if He were a heroic figure preparing for battle. This intended parallelism between pagan pathos and Christian martyrdom is of the essence, in our opinion.

This parallelism can be traced even in psychological terms. Jesus complains about His Father: "O Ye Judge of every future event . . ." (1 ff.): "Not a single day has seen me secure!" (7–8). Mary's grief for her son is said to have lasted throughout his life, for thirty years (1274). Pilate feels like an "honest exile" from Rome (358), who, although an expert in the history of law (396–420), unconsciously promotes Jewish monotheism. The crowd yells at Pilate: "Are you in charge of quelling a rebellion—did not Jesus commit *lèse-majesté* toward the emperor of Rome?" (678–80). The mob accepts the responsibility for this punishment, since there is no fair earthly judge in such a case (740). But nature also refuses to take the blame: she lets her sun suspend its orbit for a while:

If nature herself reneges on her own order, no human being, no single people, can be responsible for this evil. Either the earth will suffer a terrible disaster, or the Lord of the earth himself is in danger of losing his authority. (1132–35)

The martyrdom will come to an end by Christ's coming as the judge of all peoples (1430–31); only then will the world be truly reformed

(1431). Thus Mary, as mother of mankind, promises redemption to suffering mankind. Here the poet ends his sacred (martyr) drama with a word of hope about paradise regained.

The most deeply felt hopes are expressed in the lyrics of the choruses. His "adapting and docile genius"[31] is able to imitate Latin to a such perfect degree that the reader of the seventeenth century could easily have taken this poetry for classical rather than Neo-Latin Roman drama:

> 144 *Jam vehit praeceps per aperta noctem*
> *Mundus, et pronae properant tenebrae,*
> *Auream coelo redhibere lucem;*
> *Non tamen ductor celeris choreae*
> *Phosphorus clarum revocavit agmen,*
> *Mane nec primi roseum rubentis*
> 150 *Buccinae signum crepuere nostrae.*

> (144 By now the earth has lightened the night sky,
> and all its darkness, shadow-broken,
> paces away, but the morningstar
> leading the other stars in the night-
> watch seems still far away,
> as our Bugler does not yet
> 150 signal rose-colored daybreak.)

Nature foreshadows the arising cosmic daybreak, the New Covenant between God and man. Through Christ's (the bugler's) suffering, the paradise can be regained in heaven.

Joseph in Egypt. Grotius's third and last drama, *Joseph in Egypt* (1635), opens with Joseph's praise of the Lord ruling all over Nature (vv. 1–5):

> Once again the night vanished
> and the sun is surging out of bed
> like a young bridegroom; dressed
> in a purple robe, he raises his well-shaped head,
> and the recurring day confesses to the Lord. . . .

Here then the exiled becomes the bugler welcoming back daybreak. While Grotius was writing his drama (1633–34), his own cruelly interrupted career began to resurge, too. Two days after he had formally entered Swedish service as Chancellor Axel Oxenstierna's ambassador to Paris, he wrote to "the friend nearest to [his] heart," G. J. Vossius. He would see the drama through the press in Amsterdam. *"Sophompaneas"*—as de Groot called it by title—appeared two months after Grotius was formally introduced to his Parisian court of exile. In his introductory note (before listing the interlocutors) Grotius refers to his sources. The most prominent one is Genesis 44–45, which narrates the story of Joseph and his eleven brothers. The title is de Groot's own; he took up the *"Zophenot Paneach"* of Genesis 41:45. Although its exact meaning is obscure in the Bible, *Sophompaneas* ("he that is all-wise") approximately refers to a kind of *grand-vizier.* The plot must have been on the author's mind for quite some time. For Peter in *Christ's Passion,* vv. 265–69, alludes to young Joseph's fate and misfortunes which he received at the hands of his ruthless brothers. Unwittingly, however, they ultimately carry out God's wishes. They had become so envious of his beauty and talents, and of the preferential treatment that Joseph received from Jacob, their common father, that they threw him into an empty cistern at Dothan; when they were unsuccessful in killing him, they sold him into Egyptian servitude for twenty silver coins. According to Genesis 37:2, Joseph, at Dothan, was only seventeen, the same age Grotius was when he was advanced to second advocate of Holland, after Oldenbarnevelt in 1613. By the time de Groot wrote his last tragedy in Hamburg (as officeless exile) he had, as he confessed to Vossius, "reached that part of life . . . where a certain progress in matters of judgment is apt to show itself. . . ."[32]

In *Joseph* Grotius adroitly restricts himself to narrating the climax of the biblical *novella,*[33] and focuses his attention on the moral question and its implied legal ramifications. If the brothers had changed their ruthlessness, Joseph would be prepared to forgive them their original crime; if they had not, one of them, namely Benjamin, would have to stay behind as a slave.

Since no critical edition exists as yet,[34] it is difficult to deal adequately with this tragedy. We follow our own verse numbering, superimposed upon the original edition[35] of 1635, and interpret it without exhaustive knowledge of all the sources familiar to Grotius and his coeditor of the play. That Grotius had read Philo's *Vita Josephi* we do know for certain, however. In its final shape the drama has 1,230 lines and spreads over five acts very much as the other two plays, except that *Joseph* has a little chorus at the end, consisting of three lines, whereas the other two had no choruses in their fifth act: Act I, 233; II, 292; III, 372; IV, 243; and V, 90 verses.

The principal figures on the Egyptian side beside Joseph are the Pharaoh, who stays unnamed just as in the Bible; Ramses, chief of staff; and the chorus consisting of "Aethiopean Women." Excluding Joseph's contribution, they cover roughly one-third of the spoken material. On the Jewish side, Judah and Benjamin speak major parts in Acts II and IV (where the high points are placed). Joseph dominates all acts except the third, which is filled by indirect descriptions. Acts I and IV center totally around Joseph; Act II centers around Judah and his offer to serve as Joseph's slave (Genesis 44:18; v. 433). Act III is split in half. First, the barrenness of the rebellious "Cophtian" Country is described by a messenger; second, the splendor and bountifulness of "Memphis" are narrated by two brothers (mainly by Simeon). Grotius gave the drama less than two days and localized it, features which are both absent in the book of Genesis.

Grotius conformed in this drama to the classical Greek rules, for the action rises and falls; it rises in Act II to a first climax (433), then falls in Act III, in order to rise still higher to the absolute high point, when Benjamin offers to stay behind in Egypt as the viceroy's slave for no less than twenty years in Act IV (1076). Here Grotius clearly tries to surpass the wisdom of the Bible, but by no means in the vein of Seneca any longer. He manages this adaptation by establishing a marked parallelism between Judah's and Benjamin's moral constancy shown in adversity. The tragic situation calls for the twelfth and last offspring of Jacob and Rachel not to be outshone by Jacob and Leah's firstborn, Judah. Awestruck, his half-brother exclaims in v. 1082: "Rachel certainly gave birth to some outstanding off-spring of hers!" Here Grotius expands on the biblical text of Genesis 45:7 and makes Benjamin, rather than Joseph, shed tears at their final recognition scene, their *anagnorisis* of brotherhood. Act V glosses over the biblically required happy ending very briefly. The Pharaoh congratulates Joseph and his wife that they have such an illustrious clan in Israel. Out of thankfulness Joseph now offers to resettle his whole family, including his father,

Jacob, in Egypt. The Pharaoh in turn gives them Goshen near the Nile as lien (1167). He swears a holy oath that henceforth the Hebrew people will, according to Egyptian law, be permitted to remain in their newly adopted country as free citizens forever. He calls on the river Nile to change its water into a bloodstream if this oath is ever broken by his own successors to the throne (1197 ff.). It is Joseph's final hope that the two state religions will join and become only one, and that the Hebrew and the Egyptian law could also become one and the same. The final chorus intones: "may a celestial fire rise in the hearts of all men concerned!" (1228–30).

The poet handles his metric differentiations in a much more offhand fashion than before. One could identify metric nuances, but by and large all interlocutors, except the choruses, speak, broadly stated, in alexandrines, iambic or trochaic trimeters, and the choruses still in dimeters, as before, eleven syllables prevailing to a line. Grotius did not want to uphold the metric variety of his preceding dramas in *Sophompaneas*.

He must have noticed, and have been inspired by the fact that Joseph, the revealer of dreams and visions, lived in typological analogy to Christ. Joseph is very wise and resists temptations (Gen. 39:13 vs. Matt. 4). Christ's Jewish countrymen are envious of Him, as are the half-brothers with respect to Joseph. Both these figures are hateful for their exaltedness in the eyes of God (Gen. 37 vs. John 5:18). Both Jesus and Joseph must walk a thorny road from prison to their kingdom, Christ as "Viceroy" of God on earth, and Joseph as *"Zophenot Paneach"* (Gen. 41:43–45; 49:23 vs. Luke 24:21; Ephes. 1:22; Phil. 2:10–11). They also know the others, before they can know them (Gen. 42:8 vs. John 1:48).

But there exist also parallels and contrasts between Genesis 44–45 and 2–3 (Adam and Eve's fall) which Grotius must have hoped to capitalize on in a dramatic fashion. Both Adam and Joseph have superhuman qualities; both need to procreate on behalf of mankind. Eve is successfully tempted by the voice of sin. Joseph manages to resist the entreaties of his employer Potifar's wife (Gen. 39:7), and yet he is convicted to an undeserved term in the king's prison. Joseph, in turn, tries to deceive his brothers—by feigning a *lèse-majesté* theft of his sacrificial cup, placed in Benjamin's bag. He wants to find out whether they will seize the offered opportunity to get acquitted and sent back to their homeland—at the expense of Benjamin's life or freedom. The question the biblical narrator had to face (Gen. 44) is still the same one for the seventeenth-century dramatist: will they act again as they did at Dothan; will they resell a brother into exile, or have their characters improved ethically? Since Judah at least is prepared to give his body in lieu of Benjamin's, the peripeteia follows swiftly. Although potentially Adam's fall could be recapitulated by the brothers, resulting in extending Joseph's exile, the brothers master courage and pass Joseph's test this time. It is probably these parallels and contrasts more than personal matters[36] that attracted Grotius to the dramatization of this story. He seems to want to turn into a translator of a biblical matter, into an apologist for a reconciliation, emulating a utopian peace between Jordan and Nile. In this fashion Grotius bends a biblical novella, placed at the end of the book about the creation of the world, into a drama of recapitulating the great bugler's imperial intention of having wise government rule on earth,[37] spiritually and secularly changing exile into home.

Neo-Latin Lyrical Poetry

Special Occasion Poetry. The Tragedy *Adam in Exile* appeared in an edition with a bundle *(cumulus)* of several other sacred poems *(sacra)* and some biblical paraphrases, which will not be discussed in this book. While this "sacred poetry" was already at the printer's in April 1601, Grotius at the last moment decided to add a special ode to Easter *(carmen paschale)* commemorating his own birthday, 10 April, which in 1583 (his year of birth) had fallen on Easter Sunday. The introduction of the New Style calendar by Pope Gregory XIV, in October 1582, caused some confusion in the Netherlands, as this new dating adjustment was only accepted in two of the Dutch States (Holland and Zeeland). Thus there could be a difference of ten days depending on where one lived in the United Provinces. Due to this dating confusion, Grotius and his family made it a habit to celebrate his birthdays on each Easter Sunday. This choice gave the birthday a symbolic dimension, as it were. The Grotius clan, which had a propensity for poetry,[38] adhered to this poetic comparison to Christ's rising, an imitation particularly suited for idealizing one's entry into the world, and which might give rise to the highest expectations. The idealization also provided the young poet of eighteen with an opportunity to represent the past year in a special light, once he came of age. This auspicious connection between his own personal birth under the sign of Christ's resurrection gave Hugo Grotius leeway for poetic licence. The (New Style) calendar date indicated fortune (*fortuna* in the sense of the seventeenth century) and the parallelism to Christ's *passah* indicated the will of providence (*fatum* in the sense of the seventeenth century). Their interconnection could endow the juvenile poet with a special creative power. Quite simply stated, it gave Hugo's birthday Christ-related significance.

The ode of ninety-two lines, written in 1601, envelops the threads of fortune and fate in a circular movement. One thread is called "holy day" (*sancta lux,* v. 1), the other identified by "a life worthy of its inception at Easter" (*paschata vita,* 92), i.e., a life assuming a holy perspective. Thus Grotius prophetically anticipates at age eighteen that his further life will take a rocky course (32): "Since God gave me life at the same hour he returned it to his son (23–24), my natal hour by birth right (19) is both sacred (54) and favored (21) in the profane sense also." He would have to struggle through life not in the pursuit of happiness (58), but through an extended series of setbacks (52), remote from home (34), and yet upward-bound toward God (59–60). We cannot, however, imagine that Grotius should have believed in astrology. He vows to devote his subsequent time first of all to "sacred studies" (61–62), including sacred poetry (64), and only secondly to "profane business" (65), including profane literary works of art. He is certain of his trust in Christ, as he feels assured of his eventual rise to the heavenly Jerusalem despite proneness toward sin. The poem has a tripartite structure: I, "praise of the holy date"; II, "prayer to God"; III, consolation. Sacred studies undertaken in the spirit of Easter will save his life (61 ff., 89 ff.). The structuring seems to be inspired by Grotius's knowledge of a basic poetic formula applicable to a funerary ode or *epicedium*. Grotius applied the rule of a particular kind of ode which habitually consisted of laudation (I), lamenting (II), and consolation (III).[39] Grotius seems to console his own despair by praising the Easter hour as spiritually significant for him, and by portraying his own shortcomings during last year's achievements. He reconciles himself with his fate by vowing to study more industriously in order to compose sacred poetry.[40] His final "diamant-hard" (89) promise amounts to a self-serving prophecy: his life is illuminated by the Easter benediction, granted him at the beginning of his life. We are not overly surprised that this ode is omitted from publication in his final poetic statement, the Collected Latin Poems (= *Poemata Collecta,* TMD No. 1) of 1616, as well as the emended edition of the same collection issued in 1639. His individual assessment has been inflated to such an extent—by means of theologically unconvincing arguments—that Grotius would have invited ridicule.

The modern reader may be surprised by the almost stoic willpower expressed by the young man in this birthday ode (part III) where he states that he does not seek his fortune—despite the fact that he had already been assured of success in Leiden, Orléans, and The Hague. Instead he intends to live up to his calling, symbolized by his birthdate on Easter Sunday, by hard work of a nonprofane nature. As if he were an athlete getting ready for decisive victory, we witness a deeply religious man taking his stand. And yet the self-chosen conformity to Christianity has, even in his work, a slightly overbearing effect and perhaps sounds a little grandiloquent for a man of his age. Suffice it to say that the leading writers of his day did not express this sentiment in their praise of Hugo Grotius.

Three years later he writes his second Easter ode; this time he alludes in alcaic meter less to the Easter symbolism than to a stoic feeling of constancy in adversity. He had to lead the hectic life of a practicing attorney and of a Latin historiographer to the State of Holland.[41] The age of twenty-one ("three times seven circles," v. 5) is given structural significance in this ode. The structural division of this poem into three parts follows the poet's tripartite thought process. In the first part he relates his birthday (in manneristic fashion) to the year's cycle, only to lament: "What flight has thrown away [i.e., wasted] these sterile intermittent [twenty] years?" (6–7). In the second part, this youthful vigor is said to be yielding to fatigue. He penitently asks for God's grace, prays for the country's religious peace, and for his absolution from sin. In the third part he repeatedly asks for a spiritual rebirth (43–44). He expresses his hope that he will perform better in his legal practice (48) and as a historian (50) and that, in his spare time, he can turn his special gratitude into song (52). This ode is overladen with allusions and its imagery is no match for Grotius's first Easter song. Rather the poem *Easter 1604* reviews Grotius's past year in a conventional[42] fashion and is interlaced with evidence of growing dissatisfaction with his own "slack" performance. This self-criticism belies the fact that Grotius totally immersed himself into living up to his self-set goals. He worked through many a night in his lifetime.

The third ode is written in six-beat elegiac meter (alexandrines) and consists of 112 verses which are not arranged in strophes; e.g., *En Chrístus páritér, paritérque renáscitur ánnus* (25) ("Look, Christ is thus reborn, at the same time the year is renewed"). In v. 30 Grotius asks the self-doubting question, why can I not be congratulated on this day? (Easter 1606). The answer given: liberty (in the Netherlands) was still trampled under foot by the King (of Spain, Philip II). He wishes he could hope for an armistice, which, in reality, was still three years off. He enumerates in the further review what horrible things transpired last year, lamenting the waste of many days and nights (78). He then dedicates the following year, 1606/7, to Christ.[43] "May a holier age than the present one arrive!" (83). Finally he addresses his own personified birthday:

But you, birthday, first of our days, pardon me that I will not celebrate you [implied: with food and drink] but instead shall commemorate you spiritually. (85–86)

The ode's main thought is expressed in v. 96: "The road and the circuit of the old religion pull us in her direction." "We will not conduct a fasting, but feast by sacred joy" (i.e., by poetry). He says he will quench his spiritual thirst with the blood of Christ (103–4) and that his year (1606–7) would make him one of the true offspring of God (v. 1). As he did in his first "passaic" ode, Grotius returns to the point of departure, in order to stress the cyclical nature of an individual's calendar year.

In the spring of 1613 Grotius, as one of four delegates, was entrusted by the Dutch Government and the East Indies Company with an important ambassadorial mission to the Court of St. James in London.

Therefore, he celebrated, if celebration be the right word, his thirtieth birthday in Britain. He wrote his nonstrophic twenty-six-line fourth passaic ode in London.[44] Although Christ and his heavenly Easter light are invoked (1–2) the poem is mostly about an implied parallelism between his first mission to France[45] fifteen years ago—which failed politically—but which had netted him an honorary doctorate of law from the University of Orléans in the presence of Oldenbarnevelt, who headed the Dutch delegation. That embassy had given occasion to de Groot's first political poem (TMD 13–15), entitled *Pontifex Romanus* [The Roman Pope]. For that poem he received a gold medal from King Henry IV of France, who then dubbed him "the miracle of Holland," and another one from the States General. Bodkin argues that Grotius intended the ode to be read by King James, and that a manuscript found its way into the palace.[46]

Unfortunately the poem is disappointing—it contains no fewer than thirteen cognates of me, my, or mine—just as the conference ended in disappointment for the Dutch.[47] It could not have helped much that James was styled as the "one alone of Kings himself mightier than his own realm" (15–16). In any case, having by now seen the French and the English kings, the poet says he feels strengthened enough to accept whatever God may have in store for him in the future.

Two months later, however, it pleased the States General to appoint him governor of Rotterdam. In this position of greatest political promise Grotius reviews his own birthday for the last time, in a poem entitled *Pascha anni 1614*.

In our opinion, this final birthday ode is just as powerfully written as the first one of 1601. In his looking back on the past year the poet puts Christ's Last Supper (1–4) in parallel to Easter Sunday, as if Grotius's own *passah* demanded a special sacrifice (*piamen unum,* 2). The first unit giving the laudation, the centerpiece, so to speak, is a lamentation in which he entreats God six times with "give" (*da!*). He stylizes himself as an "accused" (*reus,* 9) having lived through "twice fifteen easterly years" (v. 10 using the *paschata* of his first ode [1.92] once again). He especially asks for "forgiveness," "firmness of character" (13; 17), "peace at home" (18), etc., until he arrives at praying for the liberty of his country (24) and "a truly Christian church" (*sacra pura,* 26) and for concord among the Dutch States (28), as if he already were the prime minister.

He even vows that he would willingly step down from office, even agree to dying, if necessary (30–31), for his office was "a yoke around his neck" (36) into which he had anyhow not been driven by "ambition" (35), and certainly not in the expectation of "financial gain,"[48] but rather because of "patriotism" (35). As in the first Easter ode Grotius returns with his last line to line one with the word "forever." For the next "twice fifteen easterly years," that is, until his death in 1645, he was to live through his birthdays in self-imposed poetic silence.[49] It is amazing to see that Grotius albeit in poetical language at age thirty-two fairly accurately predicted his own life span. In reality he had not thirty, but thirty-one more years to live.

Throughout his life, Grotius remained an ardent Dutch patriot, irrespective of the fact that The Hague government persecuted him and finally considered him a *persona non grata* among the law-abiding Dutch citizens. In particular, his patriotism expressed itself in seemingly unbreakable loyalty to the ruling House of Orange-Nassau: witness his early Greek ode of 175 verses, devoted by the twelve-year-old student-poet to the eleven-year-old fellow alumnus at the University of Leiden, Frederick Henry, the youngest son of William of Orange (1533–1584), who was to reign from 1625–1647. This poem of 1595 was only Hugo's second[50] one ever published. Thirty years later Frederick Henry (1584–1647) was not politically strong enough to pardon Hugo Grotius. Second, no fewer than fifty epigrams were devoted to Maurits of Nassau (1567–1625), William the Silent's second legitimate son and heir to the stadholdership, poems which de Groot did not stop writing until 1617, that is, until a year before Maurits's coup d'etat. In other words, we come across the startling fact that Grotius, until he was arrested in 1618, had eulogized the ruling House of Orange for fully twenty-five years. Even after his banishment had begun and become irredeemable, Grotius did not denigrate Maurits's military genius or his own former praise of Maurits's stunning victories over the Spaniards during the decade of 1590–1600. The Maurits poems listed in the *Poemata Collecta* edition of 1616 were kept in the unauthorized second edition of 1639, which appeared five years after Grotius had become a

Swedish ambassador. We do come to the conclusion that Grotius, at least on the level of poetry, was a monarch-worshiper of the House of Orange-Nassau.

Grotius precedes another one of his editions, Aratos' *Constellations* of 1600[51] by three distichs (= hexameters plus pentameters) devoted to Prince Maurits, which are a tell-tale example of flattery of high officials, typical for the Baroque Age Grotius lived in. This dedicatory poem is indicative of Grotius's early developed skill as a writer of epigrams, a literary form adapted from Greek literature, in which Grotius excelled throughout his life.[52] In his foreword, then, he praises his sovereign Maurits as follows:

In the name of Greece's first astronomer, Aratos, I dedicate to you my *Syntagma* edition (of Constellations), containing the names given to the stars in several languages. Out of humble beginnings a regal science of astronomy grew, which finally reached in you, Prince, the utter limits.[53] Edited by an as yet immature mind, this book will get into your hands whose task it is to dominate the sky, as it is your task to defeat the earth with your army.

From this point on Grotius, the as yet self-appointed state historiographer, comments in epigrammatic (Neo-Latin) form on all major victories, which Maurits, the chief admiral and general of the United Netherlands, won during the final decade of the sixteenth century.

In contrast to the above, only a single poem is devoted to Johan van Oldenbarnevelt (1547–1619) by Grotius, who was Hugo's immediate political mentor for fully twenty years. Hugo's relation to him must have been a cooler one than the one he entertained to the House of Orange. Or, as the biographer of Oldenbarnevelt, Theun de Vries, sums up his hero Barnevelt: "In many respects we may be awe-struck by him, but we cannot love him!"[54] Considering that de Groot reached the peak of his poetic productivity in the two years 1602–3, during which span he wrote almost two hundred poems, his epigram "Johan van Oldenbarnevelt" is a disappointment. It consists mainly of exaggerated flattery expressed as "best regent," "error-free," "saint," "first of the Batavians," and "Athenian officer." From reading this twenty-six-line epigram and comparing it with the Maurits poems, one gathers the obvious impression that de Groot's relation to his chief political mentor, and subsequently superior government official, must have been a very impersonal one. There is no doubt that he highly respected Barnevelt, but he did not take him for an exemplary or father figure, and there is no evidence from his poetry or his letters, as we shall see later, that Grotius "loved" Oldenbarnevelt. Perhaps Barnevelt was the kind of patriarch for whom one dared not write two eulogies. In any case, Barnevelt persuaded the government *(Gecommiteerde Raaden)* to pay Grotius a fee of three hundred guilders for the continuation of his historical research. This took place in 1603, or very shortly before this Barnevelt poem originated.

Every Grotius biographer has to live with the uncomfortable imbalance between the love letters addressed by Marie van Reigersbergh to her husband, in which she opens her heroic heart to her forever hard-working husband, Hugo, and the somewhat drier missives he sent her. (Unfortunately some may have been lost.)[55] The most moving poem of all on de Groot's wife is not by de Groot himself, but by Joost van den Vondel. This poem contains one stanza that is so beautiful that it ought to be known by heart:

> *"Een vrouw is duisent mannen t'ergh*
> *O eeuwige eer van Reigersbergh,*
> *De volgende eeuwen spreken,*
> *Hoe ghij den haet hebt uitgestreken.* (1632)

(One woman is craftier than a thousand men,
time-honored wife, Marie Reigersberghen,
let it be not forgotten for many a century
how you overcame man-made hatred triumphantly.)

And yet in 1621 Grotius wrote a funerary ode in honor of the French historian François de Thou (who had died in 1617), addressed to de Thou's son, in which he hid a prayer spoken by Marie van Reigersbergh. Here Grotius expresses in a nutshell his deep love and affection for his brave wife. He pictures her standing in his old Loevestein cell looking out of the barred window onto the river Waal below. She watches her husband, hidden in a locked bookchest, with an oxygen supply of no more than two hours before suffocating would set in, loaded on a little skiff:

Marie:
If the future which rests in you, Holiest Father, is adamantly not immovable, but you can be and enjoy being moved by prayers, accept my life-light [Hugo] whom faith of the two of us in You hid here in this chest, and liberate him from this great personal danger! As his wife I call to witness the holiest rites of matrimony and the hope of my family that I do not stay behind because I am tired of his suffering, but because I have compassion for my husband. Whatever hardships may occur, I although separated from my husband can truly bear them. If after these many intolerable hardships Your indignation will not have cooled, let it crush *me*. This live tomb shall cruelly keep and encroach upon me, and the custody of a triple wall chain me, while my Grotius will feast on fresh air, and may tell his compatriots of the hardships of his former lot.

Thus she prayed and fixed her eyes upon the sail of the skiff. . . .[56]

Of all the devotion and the support Grotius handsomely received throughout his somewhat stormy life, that rendered him by his wife, the *allerliefste* Marie, is the most touching and significant.

While Grotius was writing the history of ancient Holland at the request of the States of Holland and West Friesland, he selected some historical highlights of the battle against Spain, which had started in 1568 (and was to last until 1648), and described them in poetical form.

The most famous turning-point of that battle was the second siege of Leiden taking place in 1574, an attempt by the Spanish Generalissimo Francisco de Valdés to force the city to her knees by a tight hunger blockade. The city was defended by its burgomaster, Pieter A. van der Werff (1529–1603). Since plague and starvation were demanding a heavy death-toll from the citizens of Leiden, the heroic defender offered a crowd of mutinizing Leideners his own flesh for food. Having compared Valdés to Hannibal before the city of Zarragoza (in 219 B.C.), de Groot lets van der Werff speak the following lines:

Put your teeth into my body . . . and put an end to your hunger. I offer you . . . my throat and my limbs, which cry for their death . . . thus strengthened go on defending our city walls for a few more days, until the Prince [= Willem of Orange] will come relieving us . . . from the coast. (75–82)

This moment, when the good burghers of Leiden decline their mayor's invitation to become cannibals, is Leiden's finest and has greatly inspired Dutch patriotism. Grotius glorified it. His alma mater city was liberated a few days later, and that extra effort of heroism laid the cornerstone for the founding in 1575 of this most famous and illustrious Protestant university in seventeenth-century Europe. Here reigned freedom of thought as nowhere else in civilized Europe.

Thirty years after the liberation of Leiden, the War of Independence was still being waged by the forces of the United Netherlands. The strategically important harbor town of Ostend, after a three-year siege, was taken by the Spanish *soldatesqua* in 1604. An engraving poem by Grotius makes the suffering city talk herself, in keeping with Plutarch's opinion that a historical poem should be a "talking picture." It can be compared pictorially with the "Death Fugue" by the twentieth-century German poet P. Celan, and brings associations of Coventry, Auschwitz, and Slaughterhouse Five to the modern reader's mind. We would call *Ostenda loquitur*, therefore, the death fugue of the War of Independence, written in hexameters for the sake of invoking the fall of Troy in the *Iliad*.

Ostend talking:
The whole world watches me, a forelorn area of last-ditch defenders, still holding out proudly against the wall-ramming machines, on our coast-line which is under foreign domination.
The third year hastens to its end: three times I had to fight a new enemy. In the first place general winter whipped the North Sea, then the summer cruelly came down with the plague—the Spaniards accomplishing damage to me least of all; for a more terrible weapon is the invisible death working hand in hand with other havocs. Not one burial takes place without new people dying on the graveyard too. Death scourges me several times over . . . the question, after the enemy is beaten, is solely, who will, in dying, populate this cemetery.
The fight remaining is about occupying a sterile clod of burnt earth.

This splendid eye-witness description (as if Grotius were a war correspondent who sensed the senselessness of military destruction) is his very own specialty. There is not, to our knowledge, another Neo-Latin poet writing pictorial military history who can still move a reader of the twentieth century quite as well as Grotius here. If such a generic term were available we would call this kind of poetry military-pacifist. The topic of war and peace haunted him throughout his life, since he lived in an epoch which did not know peace, but at best only truce.

Grotius, however, not only poeticized the large national issues of the young Republic, he also had a remarkably high sense of duty toward his legal profession, despite the fact that he privately complained to his friends how little time the robe left him for writing. Let us listen to the "Office of the Advocate" speaking (1602, the poet being twenty-nine):

> Once dressed by the time-honored robe of the defense lawyer, you are entrusted with protecting the life of the accused, with protecting his fortune and his reputation. According to that trust keep your good faith, as if you were the high spokesman of the law itself; then plead the case against you through, and decide the matter as a hard pre-trial judge. Be hesitant to mete out justice according to the wishes and whims of your clients; do not consider just that what has only the outward appearance of justice. He who accepts every case, will of necessity often have to plead untruthfully [i.e. against his better knowledge].[57]

This poetic streak of Grotian self-criticism is even more pointedly put in his epigram, dated 1605, entitled "Erudite Ignorance." This pivotal sixteen-line poem leads to a climactic praise of wisdom: "A great part of absolutely certain wisdom is—not to know!"[58] Grotius is stoically talking about that which is humanly possible, and considers "a contented mind" (13–14) as pursuing only humanly possible knowledge (14). Here he may have thought of recognizing human fate in general, but in all likelihood also of the limitations of the free human will, since the poem was dedicated to a Calvinist professor of theology from Geneva.[59] If this were to be taken as someone's humanistic credo, and we believe it expresses Grotius's way of thinking about human wisdom, then whoever is convinced of it should have quit the realm of politics. Either one tended toward being erudite or one swam along with the politicians. In this world it does not seem possible to do both, as Grotius was to find out in a painful fashion. Limitations of space forbid us to delve deeper into the Grotian art of writing epigrams, the preferred genre of all of his poetry.[60]

In 1604 de Groot's younger brother Franciscus, a promising young poet (22) in his own right, died of a fever at age eighteen. Hugo writes a moving death song ("anapaestic epicedium") of 220 verses. It contains a few pieces of highly significant information on Grotius's thinking about the de Groots as a family. Great pride emanates from this eulogy of his brother, and as an expression of filial pride—the epidecium is

Poetical Works 35

technically addressed to their father, Jan de Groot—the expressions *"nostra domus"* (19); "if we are a sacred clan of de Groots to you" *(sic)* (20–21); "a titanic clan" (25) occur. Hugo must have been very fond of his young brother, as we may gather from the following excerpt:

> 93 *Dormi, dormi frater et acris*
> *Saltem sensum lucrare mali.*
> *Quanquamque feret tranquilla quies,*
> *Haec suppliciis hora peribit.*
> *Pars cruciatus vigilare fuit,*
> *Leviusque dolent quos torpor habet.*
> *Preme securo lumina somno,*
> 100 *Totumque oculis expelle diem;*

(93 Sleep, sleep my brother, so that at least the meaning of this harsh misfortune can be fathomed. Even if a windstill-lethal rest takes you away, this hour devoted to prayer will delay it. The toughest part consisted in conducting the vigil, where a cramped compassion grips those who try to alleviate their sadness. Take the candle-lights into
100 your safe sleep and banish a whole lifetime from your eyes.)

We shall now end this discussion of isolated Neo-Latin poems by Hugo Grotius. For every one chosen, two or three equally well-written ones could have been listed. But we cannot close our section on funerary odes without briefly mentioning the commemorative poem on Dr. Jacob Arminius (1550–1609), professor of theology at Leiden University (1603–9). In his three opening lines Grotius praises Arminius in vivid pictures: e.g., "deep searcher of the mine of truth"; "the budding soul of doctrine"; "the example of sharp-minded exegesis": "Now you have been taken away from this darkened century and from a half-blind crowd of palpitating sectarians; you are now inhabiting the illustrious fields of bountiful light." But then Grotius delves headlong into the polemics which surrounded Professor Arminius, while at Leiden, and even more his successor.[61] Grotius alludes to the fighting spirit of the theologians at Leiden (26) . . . "so many studies—so many deviations" (28); "Either the pestilent enemy of Christ in the black of the night implants the seeds [of discord] into the fields (29–30), or the fighting furor of mortalness and of corrupted minds will feed on any nourishment. . . ." After the exhausting fights and arguments which Jacob Arminius had to endure while lecturing at Leiden are reviewed, Grotius ends his poem: "As soon as the whole City of Christ sniffs out discord, it makes life on earth worth living, and blesses faith in heaven." Grotius took chances to point his finger at the theological factionalism at Leiden that was soon going to engulf the public mind within the whole Republic; he could not foresee that not only the bigots of his time would hold *him* partially responsible for this rift.

An Epic Legal Paraphrase. Shortly before he started working on his *Adamus Exul,* Grotius was sworn in as a lawyer in December 1599 and was appointed one of Holland's historiographers in 1601. During 1598–1600, the largest poem—other than drama—of his *Poemata Collecta,* a juridical poem of 575 hexameters, was composed.[62] These hexameters are of the dactylic variety: e.g., *Súnt quae cónstituánt hominúm patrimónia; súnt quae . . .* ("There are things that constitute the proprietor's full authority for human beings; and there are . . .").

We have to assume from the introductory lines (1–7) that the poem was originally planned in three parts (embedded into a larger work which remained unwritten), of which the present version skips the first part of the "Law of persons" as laid out in Justinian's *Institutions.*[63] The fragment that we have deals in vv. 8–118 (part II) with the "Law of corporal things" paraphrasing *Institutions,* Book I, 1, 1–10, and in vv. 119–575 (part III) paraphrasing "The acquisition of property" according to *Institutions,* Book II, 1, 11–48.

Grotius insists that his versification of Justinian's *Institutions,* the leading codified Roman law collection of all time, is not just an exercise in flattery, but "does not seem of a level inferior to [his] other poems that we displayed."[64] We think it highly significant, albeit somewhat odd, that a seventeen-year-old poet-lawyer writes a sacred drama about man's fall, and at the same time a "sacred song" partially paraphrasing a law code. In 1601, when his sacred poems were published, he must have hoped that he could finish this song in its entirety, a confidence he no longer entertained by 1616. For at that time he allowed Willem de Groot and Gerard Vossius to include the Justinian Paraphrase as a fragment of uneven proportions. In Grotius's poetry collection of 1616 this Justinian Paraphrase precedes *Christus Patiens,* thus superseding Grotius's first drama, *Adamus Exul.* We are already familiar with Grotius's low ranking of his first drama. The editor's motive for replacing *Adamus* by the Justinian Paraphrase is not that difficult to gather: in 1616 he no longer wished to be reminded of his having poeticized in a puerile fashion a Stoic-Christian epicized martyr drama. Its plot, dealing with the theft of one fruit, he had made into a case of the acquisition of unjustified, unconditional "dominance" over the whole Garden of Eden. In this paraphrase, substituted for *Adamus Exul*, he wanted to poeticize the issue of acquiring secular possession over things, from the point of view of Roman law.

We think, however, that the label "paraphrase" is not totally accurate. Grotius takes the legal prose of Justinian only as a point of departure, and winds up scanning in hexameters about the law-creating power of nature (*sanctissima . . . natura creatrix,* 15–16). We consider these paraphrasing legal hexameters stylistic exercises. The muses rather than Justinian's *Institutions* tell him their secrets about how dominance over things is to be acquired, while "the infant world was still lying in diapers" (129).

The mainstay of the poem is a paraphrase of Book II, 1, 11–48 of the private Roman law codified by Justinian, but Grotius occasionally interlaces addresses to the muses and gods and other deliberate digressions; for instance, the splendid little satire on books and the worries of their authors (421–41). Grotius satirically feigns his own fear that this booklet (436) might be used as a *fidibus* for cooking a meal on the stove. We would, however, not be justified in calling the whole fragment an exercise in legal satire. We rather take it to stand for a special kind of hexameterized chart on legal dichotomization. It seems an exercise of some undergraduate student who was anxious to learn, in the shortest possible time, Justinian's argument on categorizing and acquiring property by making use of the weapon of wit, including mock self-deprecation—the muses remember everything (121)—so why not us?[65]

Contrary to the last word used in Grotius's title, *"dominium,"* the poem does not reach such a level of abstraction. It does not deal with the notion of property in an abstract way, but rather with the practical question of who owns what under which particular circumstances. The poet uses *dominus* ("proprietor") dozens of times. Not before 1604, however, does Grotius develop a systematic notion of the basic legal faculty of *dominium.*[66]

Collected Poems (= Poemata Collecta). Except for one ecclesiastic treatise[67] which appeared in 1617, Grotius's collected poetry edition of 1616 constitutes his last major literary accomplishment before he was arrested in August 1618. In a fashion its appearance marks the end of Hugo's youthful, more enthusiastic occupation with *belles lettres*. The collection was seen through the press by his nineteen-year-old brother Willem. He was assisted in this task by the experienced thirty-nine-year-old professor G. J. Vossius. In fact, Grotius himself decided which poems should be included and which ones should be dropped.[68] The arrangement and the contents of this Neo-Latin collection are as follows; the bulk of the sacred and lyric poems fall into four parts; first, three books of *silvae,* occasional poems having strophic units of seven or eleven syllables; second, one book of elegies; and third, three books of light verse medley poems, so-called *farragines;* and fourth, two books of (290) epigrams of eight, ten, twelve, or more verses in Part One, and two-line epigrams in Part Two.

The oldest of these poems reaches as far back as 1595; there is another one of 1598, a few more from 1599, and others after 1610; but the bulk were written during the first decade of the seventeenth century.[69] So we find some 373 medium- to larger-sized Neo-Latin poems in the whole collection, encompassing twenty years of writing and more than ten thousand lines of poetry.

The sacred and lyric poems are followed in the sequence by the 875-line *Justinian Paraphrase,* the Consolation Oratory written on the occasion of Franciscus Grotius's death, and the 1432-line drama *Christus Patiens.* A comparison to his own sacred poetry having been written and partially published before 1608 shows that Grotius did not wish his poetic New and Old Testament paraphrases to be included in this 1616 poetry edition. Also quite a few of his (private) occasional poems, mainly consisting of epicedia and of epithalamia, as well as his youthful Greek poetry, were omitted. Someone had his *Poemata* collection reedited in 1639. This unauthorized printing contains basically the same material as in 1616, except for a greatly enlarged second part of epigrams, and the addition of the third drama, *Sophompaneas,* as well as the *Silva* addressed to Thuanus, discussed above. All these addenda swelled the number of verses of the first edition, 12,800, to about 15,000 in the second.

Dutch (= Nederduitse) Poetry

Considering the date of publication, 1616, it appears that Grotius collected his Neo-Latin poetry rather late in his poetic career; as a

Poetical Works

matter of fact only after his creativity had declined. He did not seem to collect or have collected his Dutch poetry during his life time. With one exception it began to appear after his death in the second half of the seventeenth century. And yet, twenty sacred and seven secular *Nederduitse* poems by Grotius, encompassing 8,123 lines, exist, most of them written while Grotius was a government prisoner at Loevestein. It is significant that the prisoner in his isolation should temporarily cry out his pain[70] in his mother tongue rather than in the humanist idiom of his age. We will come back to this temporary linguistic choice and its consequences for the assessment of Grotius's personality in Chapter 6 of this study. Similar to his Neo-Latin poetry, his Dutch poetry falls into two categories, sacred and secular. First we shall cast a quick glance at the small number of secular Dutch poems.

Secular Poems. The more than seventy carefully chiseled Neo-Latin epigrams on Maurits, printed in pamphlets, collections, and on etchings and engravings, could not, in our opinion, make up for the *one* Dutch poem consisting of twenty-two couplets entitled "Complaint by the Lady of Mechelen over the Love of the Prince of Orange." This poem apparently circulated at Court in The Hague, in all likelihood without immediately giving Grotius away as the author (assuming he really was the author as alleged in 1651 by four anonymous editors).[71] Nowadays it is available in the rare edition of Jeronimo de Vries.[72]

This eighty-eight–line alexandrine poem falls into five parts: first, a general lachrymose complaint by the forsaken woman;[73] second, a direct address to Maurits, the unfaithful lover; third, an admonition to her "sweet children"; fourth, a moral plea to all girls involved in illicit love affairs; and finally an epilogue of two couplets (20–21).

The varied allusions to, e.g., "Icarus" and his crash landing, to her "lost honor," to Maurits's "unsteadiness," but particularly couplet 17, "until you find another woman in love comparable to me, but of higher lineage, who will be honored by you, without experiencing shame or fright, and who will stay with you permanently" (lines 65–68) we consider highly denigrating to the prince. If (before 1618) Maurits had ever been informed who the author of this invective was, he would have had cause to hate this arrogant writer for having trespassed the threshold of literary taste. In any case, the devastating effect of these eighty-eight lines of Dutch poetry would have destroyed the goodwill seemingly created by the 350-odd lines of elegant Neo-Latin epigrams, which highly praise the official Maurits in military action and glory.

What good could the idealization do, if de Groot's real view of his sovereign was expressed thus in his mother tongue?

Religious Epic: *True Religion*. In a letter written to his (five[74]) children sometime early in 1631 Grotius reminisces about his Dutch literary endeavors while imprisoned at Loevestein: "I sought to honor and display our Nether-Dutch mother tongue."[75] The "six books" remark refers to the six chapters of the *Bewijs van de waeren Godsdienst* [Proof of True Religion], written in four months, from December 1619 to April 1620. But de Groot had already praised the merits of the Dutch language as a full-fledged vehicle of communication in comparison to the "classic" Renaissance language of the century, Latin, as early as 1602,[76] and was merely repeating a stance taken under different circumstances twenty years before. For Grotius was, in a sense, not only the disciple of J. J. Scaliger and other outstanding professors of literature at Leiden; at a very early age he was the collaborator and translator[77] of the famous mathematician Simon Stevin (1548–1620), a friend of Grotius's father, Dr. Jan de Groot, and of Maurits van Nassau. Stevin was the author of the epoch-making volume *Elementary Mechanics* (1586), which contained in its preface a famous apology for using the Netherlandic (= Dutch) language, a rather bold step at that time. This treatise was familiar to Grotius.[78]

Grotius gives the prospective reader of *Bewijs van de waeren Godsdienst* an apology of the truthful Christian religion, his reasons why his didactic poem *(gedenck-geschrift)* had to be written in Dutch rather than in Latin verse: he addresses his poem to the Dutch seamen, a large, but of course largely fictitious missionizing readership of several thousands, who came into contact with many men abroad.[79] It is of course possible that Grotius wanted the reader to associate his "ship" with the church of Christ, and the mast with the cross Christ had to bear, and seamen had to bear in foreign countries:

> Vv. 1 Trouhartigh Hollandsch volck/
>   vermaert van meenig eeuw/
>   Die nu al over langh de vlagghe van de Leeuw
>   Doen vlieghen hebt soo verr' de wind heeft konnen draghen/
>   End uwen naem verbreyd/ soo daer't begint te daghen/
>   Als daer den avond rijst/. . . . (TMD 144)[80]
>   (Trustworthy Hollandic People,

> Famous for many centuries,
> who have carried the Flag of the Lion for so long now
> into the four corners of the world as far as the wind
> has carried you, and who have spread your reputation from
> Orient to Occident. . . .)

These alexandrines swell as sails carrying the wind of Christian good tidings everywhere—even the title is versed accordingly: Bewíjs van de wáeren Gódsdienst in sés bóecken ghestélt. It contains 4,798 vv. in six chapters or, counted differently, in 120 blocks of irregular length.

Books I–II arrange the Christianity-attesting narrative materials; Books IV–VI, the Christianity-denying material. Each block is graced by a marginal comment, as if the reader dealt with a theological tract matter rather than a poem. The whole of nature, as a matter of belief, attests to the veracity of the Christian religion; the pagan idolatries, on the other hand, contrary to their intention, attest to this truth also, as do the carefully chosen and numerous allusions to outstanding pagan philosophers and Christian church fathers. The errors in writing on the pagan side seem to corroborate the gospel of Christ. Book I specifically deals with God and religion in general; Book II, with proofs adducable for the truth of Christian religion; Book III, with the overbearing weight on the scale of truth because of the belief in the Holy Scriptures, and mainly of the New Testament (a neat circular argument by Grotius). Book IV discusses the main characteristics and sources of pagan religion (in parallelism to Book I); Book V contains a polemic against Judaism—which is, however, by no means anti-Semitic[81]— Book VI is directed against the Muslim religion. Vivid pictorial images are often set off against each other fugally, i.e., mannesristically. Both halves carry a theme. The first half carries the main theme toward a high point, the truth attained by Christianity. The second half carries the subordinate theme, indirectly praising God. The belief expressed is both naive and rationalistic—and at times lawyerlike—a belief using a missionary ideology. As everybody may intuitively understand the underlying structure of a Baroque fugue, without realizing its detailed intricacies, so can the reader of Grotius's most popular epic poem enjoy the representation, be he a Catholic, a Lutheran, a Calvinist, or even a Greek-Orthodox. Catholic friends of his persuaded him to translate his *Bewijs* into Latin. He accomplished that task in Paris and published his own Latin version, *De Veritate Religionis Christianae*,[82] in Leiden and Paris that same year, 1627. The epilogue is very moving:

> v. 4788 Neemt niet onwaerdigh aen dit werckstuck
> mijner handen/
> O des aerdbodems merckt/ o bloem der Nederlanden/
> Schoon Holland: laet dit sijn in plaets van mÿ by u
> Mÿn' Coningin: ick thoon so als ick kan noch nu
> De liefde die ick heb altÿd tot u ghedraghen
> En draegh en draghen sal voorts alle mÿne daghen.
> Vind ghy hier iet het welck u dunckt te wesen goed/
> Bedanckt hem sonder wien gheen mensch iet goeds en doet.
> Is hier of daer ghemist/ erinnert met meedooghen
> U selven wat een Wolck bedwelmt der menschen ooghen:
> Verschoont veel liever't werck dan dat ghÿ't bitter laeckt
> 4799 En denckt/ och Heer/ het is te Loevestein ghemaeckt.

(Do not take this creation of my hands as unworthy, and do not overlook from which soil it sprang, o flower of the Netherlands, o beautiful Holland: let this poem be with you instead of me, my Queen, I show as I still may now, the love I have always harbored for you, feel, and will feel for the rest of my days. If you should find here something which you will consider well done, thank Him, without whom no human can perform any good at all. If I missed a point here or there, please be mindful with compassion and try to visualize what a cloud is overshadowing man's vision. Be merciful in criticizing my work rather than bitterly repudiating it; and remember, O Lord, it has been made at Loevestein Prison.)

Between this heart-moving epilogue and the prologue we quoted above, the thoroughly undogmatic main body of this poem rolls forward in an artistic wave. Could Grotius, seemingly imprisoned for life, foresee that this poem was destined to become a kind of *vademecum* of educated Christians all over the world for about three hundred years? The outstanding line of the *Bewijs* is perhaps v. 360: "For between good and evil a freedom of choice is placed." This stoic pièce de resistance indicated Grotius's thinking about God. Grotian Christianity in its widest sense has become a *primus inter pares* religion without being fixed on any one confession or strict dogma.[83]

Consensus in a common tradition and belief in the truth of Christian miracles form the poetized basis of the Grotian belief system, which is open to inquisitive analyses from all ages, but is not marked by gnawing doubts. Naturally, the mysteries of Christianity are not subjected to poetic debating. The higher Christian morale is being sanctified in a beautifully flowing seventeenth-century Dutch, surpassed—as far as the alexandrine verse is concerned—by no other Dutch writing in the first half of that century.

With this poem, ironically not originally written in the language of European humanism, but rather in rhythmically pictorial Dutch, Hugo Grotius entered the realm of bilingual world literature. His stoic-Christian epic in six books from Loevestein spread his fame to every corner of the globe and was translated into twelve languages.[84]

Chapter Three
Philological Text Editions

Greek or Latin Poetic Texts

The Seven Liberal Arts by **Martianus Capella.** Many centuries ago, the "seven liberal arts" and the "seven sisters" meant one and the same thing, namely the seven disciplines: grammar, dialectic, rhetoric, geometry, arithmetic, astronomy, as well as spheric or musical harmony. These were the subjects worth knowing.

In the fifth century A.D. an old Roman lawyer by the name of Martianus Capella wrote a satire *(Satyricon)* which is commonly referred to as "The Seven Liberal Arts, or: The Wedding of Mercury and Philology." This Latin prose/verse medley is written as an allegory and surprisingly became Western Europe's leading textbook until the seventeenth century. Hugo Grotius ardently read it in the edition of Bonaventura Vulcanius (Basle 1577) when he was thirteen, deciding, at the insistence of his teacher at Leiden, J. J. Scaliger (who did not care to edit it himself, but intended to assist his star pupil), to gain philological distinction with a new edition. Although it took Grotius three years to see it through the press working in his spare time, due to his prolonged stay in France in 1598–99, it finally saw the light of day in 1599.[1]

Let us now peruse the contents (first of Book I and II) of our satirical encyclopedia of heathen "knowledge." Mercury, after some unsuccessful attempts to secure a suitable wife for himself, consults his brother Apollo, who advises him (in hexameters, of course) to woo the maiden Philology, a most erudite virgin, and daughter of Wisdom (Phronesis). Mercury obtains his marriage recommendation from Virtue. In the Council of those Gods who have senatorial rank, a resolution is passed eventually to promote the bride to the ranks of the immortals.

At the threshold of Heaven, Philology is given a special brew. Upon drinking it, she disgorges her mental burden, that is, she vomits a whole library out of her bowels, a library in all seven disciplines, eagerly rubricated and professionally shelved by the liberal arts, her bridesmaids. Thereupon lady Apotheosis renders the bride a second cup. Its sweet draught bestows immortality upon Philology and gives her equal standing with her bridegroom, Mercury.

After this initiation ritual she is transported up the Milky Way till the entourage reaches the Seat of the Gods. Everybody is assembled to greet them: Mercury's fellow deities, the various sons of Jupiter, Linus (the son of Apollo), Homer, Virgil, Orpheus making melody, Pythagoras, Euclid, Plato rolling golden spheres, Thales, Aristotle, Epicur, Zeno, etc., in short, more than a hundred guests. Now the ladies "constituting a dower" are presented as handmaidens to Mercury's bride. Each of them, for entertainment's sake, is asked to describe the principles of her own discipline. The following chapters, Books III to V, encompass the speeches of the so-called trivium (= the three-way subjects of the liberal arts, considered easier for the novice to master), and Books VI to IX, the so-called quadrivium, considered the "hard" educational subjects in the Middle Ages.

"Grammar and Literature," Book III, descendant of the Egyptian God Osiris, is represented as an old gray-haired Greek woman, dressed in a Roman cloak symbolizing that the Latin grammatical tradition depended heavily on her Greek mistress. She carries an ebony casket containing surgical instruments for operating on children committing grammatical errors. With her charm she can remedy faulty speech and restore truth. "Dialectic," Book IV, steps forward, taking Grammar's place; she is of plain complexion, intelligent, but with keen, somewhat shifty eyes and dark curly hair; a serpent is coiled in one of her hands, and in the other, waxen tablets are placed, hooked to draw men toward the serpent's bite. With a parting shot she makes way for Rhetoric.

"Rhetoric," Book V, who is of outstanding beauty, very tall, self-confident, and bouncy, is described as being golden-voiced and of prodigious memory. The force of her arms is like a bolt sent by Jupiter; she could do nothing discreetly. "Geometry," Book VI, despite her look of distinction, represents foremost geography; her face is shining with mystery, as she is able to describe every position on the earth's surface accurately from memory. But as soon as she must lecture on the less familiar subject of geometry, she hastily snatches the lecture notes away which Euclid holds in his hands. "Arithmetic," Book VII, is a lady of majestic appearance; ten rays appear on her brows, ten being the basis of all human calculation; her counting fingers can vibrate at tremendous speed; she is the first one not asked to stop her presentation, but ends out of her own free will. "Astronomy," Book VIII, is presented as a beautiful Romanized maiden hailing originally from Athens; her brows are starlike; she arrives in a flash of light; she wears whirring wings and holds a sextant in her hands; Mercury trained her in this ancient art of pathfinding. Since the standbys "Medicine" and "Architecture" (the eighth and ninth liberal arts) are mainly concerned with mortal men on earth, they are left out of the presentations. The last speaker, allowed to end the learned charade, is "Spheric Harmony," Book IX, the darling of the heavens, actually the twin sister of arithmetic; her dress is adorned with laminated gold, and her intelligence is extraterrestrial. She can make mortal and divine music, and in the end hums a lullaby in front of the bridal chamber.

Grotius read this medley poem ". . . as it was intended [by Capella] to be read for edification and amusement. He read Latin as if it were his vernacular. . . ."[2] Grotius could appreciate the mannberistic, if slightly barbaric, propensities of the work: he learned to handle the fifteen various classical meters[3] employed by Capella; he could delve deeply into Greek mythology, satire, and he could discern the masters which were the African medleyer's principal sources, Cicero, the rhetor, Virgil, the poet, Varro, the grammarian, and Pliny, the natural historian.[4] These and Klio (history), Melpomene (tragedy), and Oerania (astronomy), accompanied "young Hugo, the state historian-to-be, the incipient dramatist," and the translator of works on astronomy[5] for part of his life. This satire left an indelible stamp on Grotius's mind which was ever rapidly widening into encyclopedic proportions. Henceforth he adapted the Capellan method of intermingling prose and poetic quotation, particularly in his main juridical works, but above all in *Law of War and Peace*.[6] He also learned that there was a didactic method of presenting learning material, by which students learned their texts without going to the original sources. For various reasons, Grotius did not ever aspire to a professorship at Leiden, Paris, or elsewhere, as he confessed in a letter addressed to his father.[7] For the educational theories of his days were only a fraction less confusing than those of a Martianus Capella: they were still receptive and ultimately a mixed bag, notwithstanding that at Leiden the offerings were mixed more judiciously than anywhere else in Europe at that time.[8] On the other hand, he did not refuse editing this satire, as it was comfortably ". . . uniting peoples in one common fellowship of the Church. . . ."[9] His conjectures were praised by the literary public. Ironically, thirteen years after the appearance of his masterful and highly appreciated first edition, it was put on the Index of Prohibited Books by the Spanish Inquisition.[10]

Constellations & Weather Signs by Aratos of Soloi. The French lyricist Pierre de Ronsard, who died in 1585, once complained in an ode to his lackey (*Odes* 2:18) that "my mind has been bored to tears having studied the *Phainomena*[11] by Arat too hard." The modern reader need not sympathize with his sigh, since nowadays annotated bilingual editions are readily available.[12] Grotius based his 1600 edition on G. Morel's (Paris, 1559). The next editor, J. Schwarz (Coburg, 1715), printed many of the conjectures Grotius had proposed but had not put in his text himself.

Arat of Soloi (in Cilicia, Greece) lived from 315 to 245 B.C. and wrote his didactic poem *Phainomena* in Greek hexameters, probably in 275. His poem was used as a schoolbook for centuries. Virgil based his *Georgics* (particularly Book I) on Arat.[13] M. T. Cicero (106–43 B.C.) translated the *Phainomena* into Latin. The poem of 1,154 hexameters consists of two main parts, the first one pretending to address itself to peasants (vv. 1–757, tr. τα ουράνια, treating astronomical matters). In this first part Arat describes constellations of the firmament between heaven and moon in the position of rest. In the second part, vv. 758–1154, the so-called Μετέωρα (pretended to have been written for sailors), the rotating firmament between heaven and earth is described in such a way that natural phenomena become "weather signs," almost an almanac's forecasting system. One verse (5) of the opening invocation addressed to Zeus has the honor of being quoted verbatim by St. Paul in Acts 17:28: "We too are God's children." The poem does not simply contain confused bits of half-education. Rather it attempts to show that Zeus's weather forecasts are signs which can be made use of if properly interpreted. These signs can be observed in the moon, the sun, and the stars, clouds, fog, animals strutting, etc. Vv. 909–1043 are of particular concern to coastal dwellers and seafarers such as the inhabitants of Holland. The second *meteora* part sings of objects in rotation, mostly the signs of the zodiac. Here Arat can either increase the tempo of his description or slow it down, so that W. Ludwig speaks of a "contrapuntal and yet symmetrical variation of the narrative tempo,"[14] particularly in vv. 480 ff. Arat furthermore glides over changes from one paragraph to the next, associating rather than rubricating different subjects.

De Groot critically edits the main poem by Arat, and three translations into Latin, one by Cicero, one by Germanicus Caesar,[15] and one by an obscure Roman writer, Avienus. The translation of Germanicus is illustrated by the engraver and etcher J. de Gheyn. These are etchings of constellations, planets, and seasons in miniature with a long iconographical background carefully mapped by A. W. Byvanck.[16] The inclusion of such maps and the interruption of the hexameters by the Grotian prose comments, show that the edition was meant to edify to a degree of high usefulness, but was not intended as a strictly scientific pamphlet. That is not to say that the two editors (de Groot and de Gheyn) considered their astrological material totally unscientific. Grotius was a trained Aristotelian and Ptolemaean, not a Copernican. He most likely did not wish to imply that his basic text[17] contained up-to-date natural history as taught at the University of Leiden around 1600. Rather, he was convinced that the poem attested to the greatness of Zeus, and hence of God, by poetical observance of practical phenomena. To make the text as clear as possible he chose to have it illuminated with material compressed into *one* time perspective. This material, actually gathered and collected for over a thousand years, was inserted between the hexameters. The publisher must have been convinced that the information value of such a collection was high. It was reprinted with some modifications in five different countries until the nineteenth century. The States of Holland were interested enough to pay their historiographer-to-be the sum of 300 guilders.

The style of this illustrated didactic poem is manneristic and betrays the spirit of joy in conglomerating various pictorial, astronomical, and poetic sources, and thus contributes toward the renaissance theory of education by example. (It was therefore put on the Index of Prohibited Books, too.) This illustrative comparison of drawn and etched objects in rest and in motion called for employing the language of humanistic learning, Latin, in prose and in verse. Weather forecasting was an art of particular relevance for the chief admiral of the fleet, Maurits van Nassau. We are not surprised that a special copy was dedicated to him.[18] From working on this edition, Grotius perfected his skill in Greek and Latin; he learned to "paint" objects, and he became assured of displaying the learning of other ages. In short, he mastered the art of encyclopedizing facts and interpretations. He could from now on depict the universality of times,[19] and the temporality of motions in a somewhat manneristic fashion. At the threshold of the seventeenth century the Netherlands possessed in Grotius their most versatile writer. He could verbally describe the burghers of his time, but he could also characterize men of other ages. Henceforth he embodied The Hague's most promising talent of the literary republic.

Greek Texts with Latin Translations. While Grotius was waiting in The Hague Prison for his trial to begin (during which time his son Diderik was born) he started to translate two voluminous Greek collections containing thousands of once famous and useful quotations from four hundred poets.[20] The collection was originally put together by the Macedonian Joannes of Stoboi (Stobaeus) in about A.D. 500. Grotius managed to get it finished by 1 February 1620,[21] and published it, after his escape, in Paris, April 1623. Stobaeus's arrangement is by subject rather than by author, spread over four books. The first two contain excerpts from Greek writers on natural philosophy and logic. Books three and four have the character of an anthology. The main topic of the first two books is morals; the subjects of the latter ones, politics, economy, and art.[22] The most frequently quoted literary authors in all four books are Euripides, Menander, Plato, Plutarch, Sophocles, and Xenophon.[23]

By translating *Sententious Dictions* the captive attorney general continued the encyclopedically oriented work he began as a private citizen. His translation is not only concise, but it has the attraction of displaying poetic opinions of many ancient writers whose writings would otherwise have been lost. Those writers whom Stobaeus did not include, our savant translator collected separately by author in excerpt form.[24]

In his Introduction or *Prolegomena* to his *Phoenissae* edition (TMD no. 496) Grotius tells the prospective reader of this drama by Euripides (in

Latin translation) that he as editor and translator derived "a moral remedy" from reading Greek tragedies by Euripides (480–406 B.C.) at Loevestein prison. Whereas Grotius's former friend Daniel Heinsius, in his treatise *The Essence of Tragedy*[25] of 1611, had considered Sophocles (496–406 B.C.) the champion of the tragic style, and had recommended him as a model to imitate, he had also voiced his opinion that the decline of Greek drama had set in with Euripides, ". . . as a result of the negative influence of Greek sophistry on the purity of thought and expression."[26]

Hugo Grotius took up that gauntlet in his Introduction, breaking a lance for his preference for Euripides. Had, after all, Aristotle himself not named Euripides' dramas the most tragic of Greek tragedies?[27] He tries to advance reasons to correct Heinsius's lopsided preference for Sophocles. Tragedy, he begins, takes first place in all of the various disciplines of poetry, and Euripides undoubtedly takes first place among the Greek dramatists; and the *Phoenician Maidens* is dubbed the most outstanding of Euripides' eighteen tragedies. This judgment is purely personal and clearly biased, for he bases his preference on no more than "the judgment of the old grammarians" and on his own translations of three of the eighteen dramas. For he himself is of the opinion that "the emotional cleansing effect" (catharsis) is strongest felt by Eteocles', the protagonist's, speeches on the problems of law and legitimacy of power as dramatically and philosophically outstanding. For Heinsius, on the other hand, the type of the returning son of Oedipus (Eteocles) was "too intellectual."[28] At the end of his Introduction, however, Grotius admits that Sophocles *is* superior in respect to dramatic "sense," "weight," and "majesty"; but still Euripides, in his eyes, was "perspicuous," and more "elaborated." Apparently Grotius liked one feature of the *Phoenissae* best, namely "temporal spacing" *(temporis spatium),* a technique by which the two hostile brothers, Eteocles and Polyneices, advance their reasons as to why they have to engage in war. This reasoning makes the *Phoenician Maidens* a legal drama which Grotius would have preferred to call the (hostile) *Brethren of Thebes*.[29]

For de Groot three separate Greek-Latin editions formed a "brotherhood": the Stobean *Dictions,* the *Excerpts* from Greek tragedies and comedies (1626), and the Greek *Epigram Anthology,* the most ambitious translation ever undertaken by Grotius. According to the bibliographers Ter Meulen and Diermanse (TMD 534 note 8), Grotius performed this gigantic task of translating some 2,400 epigrams in exactly one year (at the rate of 200 epigrams a month) and was the first one to translate them into Latin in full. We do think that this is not humanly possible, and that Grotius must have started on that project shortly after 1603. In any case, his translation was ready to be printed, but ever since 1634 he wanted it printed face to face, with the original text. No publisher dared to undertake such an ambitious and perhaps nonrewarding foray. For these and many other unfortunate reasons the bilingual publication did not appear until 1795, and even then it took twenty-seven years to complete the job.

Notwithstanding its modest title, the Greek anthology is a work of stupendous diligence and giant proportions. It encompasses the work of no less than twenty major epigrammatic schools from 650 B.C. to A.D. 550. It is not really the work of one man, or of one collecting generation, but of the whole Greek genius as it expresses itself throughout 1,200 years. Thus it represents in a fashion an epigrammatic history of its own, and gushes forth thousands of shades of Greek and Hellenistic wit amidst political terror; it contains archaic humor in a nutshell. The epigram became versed in the eighth century B.C., usually in the form of trimeters or hexameters, originally in one line only, around 500 B.C. The (two-lined) distich becomes the form of the epigram par excellence. The Greeks had defeated the Persians, hence the poetic image of themselves rose considerably, just as Dutch pride was swelled by the relief of Leiden (New Athens) in 1574 and the victory at Nieuwpoort in 1600.

Gradually the epigram collection shifts its emphasis from epigrams engraved in stone to those written for books. In this process the realm of persons greatly increased until slaves and children could be epigrammatized (i.e., heroic), too. Various successive Greek schools mixed theology, satire, as well as didactic and philosophic elements into the epigram. The epigram collection of Planude (the monk Maximos Planudes lived in the fourteenth century A.D.) is already the seventh major collection of this kind of Greek poetry. It contains moral, satirical, religious, and erotic inscriptions of all kinds for all occasions in some 15,000 verses.

The first epigram collection in Western Europe appeared in 1474, the first scientifically adequate edition in 1566. The first Latin prose translation was rendered by P. Manutius in 1574, but it has never been published. The first bilingual Greek-Latin edition is by Eilhard Lubinus and appeared three times in Heidelberg during 1603–4, exactly the time when Grotius started to show interest in the Greek epigram. Whether Grotius used this forerunner could not be ascertained by us, but it seems likely.[30] Grotius liked very much the baroque and sophisticated element in the postclassical epigram, e.g., by Kallimachos (*Anthologia Graeca,* v. 146): The New Statue of a Grace:

> Of Graces in number are four, for added to three thus far
> a new one was created, humid of glittering oil.
> She beams before others on earth, the lucky Berenika,
> without her grace, graces would not be Graces at all.

Reflections on Fate and Free Will by Various (Mostly Greek) Philosophers.[31] Grotius excerpted sentences from several schools of philosophical thought (Pythagoraean, Platonic, Peripatetic, Stoic, Epicurean, Jewish, and Christian Schools). He chose thirty-one philosophers who were predominantly Greek, but also Roman, and collected their sayings in an anthology of his own. The edition is loosely structured around twelve chapters and one fragment. He translated the gist of their positions into Latin, as far as it seemed profitable to him. The title is actually a double one: "About fate and that which is in our power."

As for J. J. Scaliger, fate for Grotius was a dark, unfathomable power. A lighted spot in this darkness was formed by Christian providence, recognizable behind the fortuitous, the mere $αδιάφορον$, as the Stoics called it. The editors of TMD could not determine how far back Grotius started to collect such statements. Considering the volume we think that it must have been a long time. We also suppose that Vossius must have helped Marie van Reigersbergh with the preparation and the dedication. Unfortunately our Elzevier-Amsterdam edition lacked an *argumentum* (contents summary), so we are inclined to suppose that this syllabus had not reached final publishable form.

Grotius, in any case, combines in this posthumous work the historic and the thematic approach for the first time. The various chapters summarize positions by philosophical schools as he interpreted them. The phrase "that which is in our power" (reason) is included time and again in his subsequent subheadings. The dialectically opposed notions of fate and willpower could also be termed blind force (alleviated by providence) versus human virtue. From reading some of these chapters we gathered the impression that Grotius did not mean to have these antipredestination "confessions of a humanist" published in this present form. They deal in their entirety with his personal concordance, as it were, on philosophical positions which are always mindful of its opposite *(audiatur et altera pars)*. We do detect the arranging hand of the legal mind, but not its usual acumen.

The reader may gather what kind of consolation the philosophers discussed by Grotius had to offer, if pressed about the range of their definitions. We think the collector ultimately had a commentary in mind, not an annotated paraphrase on fate. Grotius carefully abstains from giving either side (fate or free will) too much credence. At times, particularly at the beginning of several of his chapters, the reader is made to believe that he is witnessing a sermon in essay format. We find elements of Montaigne and Lipsius in the Grotian "fragment." Lipsius in his *Physiologia Stoicorum* (1604)[32] had taught that there was no real difficulty in reconciling the Stoic notion of *fatum* with the Christian emphasis on the free will of man as ordained by God. Right reasoning, although as a principle it is inborn, could nonetheless be acquired by training. Being skeptical and believing at the same time was still possible. Be that as it may, the illustration technique seems quite Lipsian. The key to understanding this entanglement may be found in the subtitle of the work, "collected in part by Hugo Grotius." Before a definitive judgment on the literary origin of the whole collected material can be rendered, it must be pointed out here that Grotius's personal convictions are carefully hidden under the cloak of philosophical positions of different schools of thought. We surmise that this essayistic discourse on fate may contain more of Grotius the polyhistorian than of Grotius the virtuous adaptor.

Latin Historic Texts

***Civil War* (Pharsalia) by M. L. Lucanus.** "Grotius in particular loved his Lucan which he always carried in his pocket, and was in the habit of kissing it often."[33] Although the story may be apocryphal, Grotius did study Lucan's epic repeatedly since 1607. The love of liberty and the hatred of tyranny expressed by this Cordoban Roman, Lucan (A.D. 39–65), a senator living in Rome at the time of Nero, recommended him to the Dutchman, who managed to publish his critical edition with Raphelengius at Leiden in April 1614, at the same time that he also wrote his last passaic ode.[34] Based on the work of several predecessors, Grotius edited the *Pharsalia* (as it is traditionally called after the battle description of Book VII, which depicts a historic battle between Caesar and Pompey in 48 B.C.). Grotius performed such a thorough job that the most recent edition still quotes some of his emendations.[35]

"We sing of war far worse than civil . . . and of legality confirmed on crime. . . .": thus begins Book I, in obvious allusion to Virgil's *Aeneid*. Lucan was convinced that his poem would eventually converge the fame of Pompey, who fought the Battle at Pharsaly (Thessalony, Greece), and of himself, who recorded it in poetic writing, as he proudly says in Book IX, 985–86 ("The Battle of Ph. will live eternally and no subsequent Age will ever condemn us to oblivion!"). In ten books (of, most likely, twelve, had Lucan finished his fragment) the various and mostly gloomy aspects of the civil war fought between father-in-law Caesar and son-in-law Pompey are presented in manneristic and sometimes gory detail. This deliberately anti-Virgilian epic moves like a fully drawn battleship, all sails atop. The patriotic subject, the survival of Rome's glory, is tragic. The liberty of Rome is being victimized by the vicious conqueror and murderer Caesar *(parricida),* who is compared to Hannibal the Phoenician. In passionate diction the poet displays such anti-Caesarian partisanship throughout the whole poem. He certainly has an axe to grind! He depicts his rival's defeat by means of a paradoxical imagery that may have been influenced by stoicism, and above all by the teachings of the philosopher M. S. Seneca, his very powerful uncle at Rome. (Soon they were both forced to commit suicide by their disenchanted emperor, Nero.)

The decline of Rome and her fall into cosmic catastrophe is sealed in Book VII, the battle description of Pharsaly, whence Pompey the formerly Great was forced to flee in unstoic haste. At that time, Lucan suggests, liberty was forced to forsake Rome, so that Rome could no longer play the role of capital of the world. Thus the door to "ancient chaos" was opened once more; consequently Lucan interprets that decisive battle in terms of a riot, a furor—in short, a crime *(nefas)*.

It is clear from reading the Latin text why it appealed so much to Grotius: it represents an epic narrative of tragic proportions with an impact for all times, its pivotal message being the destructive consequences of civil war! It furthermore displays a giant match between fortune, tilted in Caesar's favor, and fate, crushing the old hollow oak Pompey like a bolt of lightning. The giant fight was to invite the reader to judge "a criminal action" as if before a court. There is no ironic distance between the narrative matter and the epic storyteller Lucan. His language is *recherché* and manneristic to the point of paradox. Lucan reaches an absolute crescendo when he depicts floods, storms, and battle scenes. He describes something very dear to weather-minded Dutchmen: a Spanish flood (Book IV, 48–120); an Italian seastorm (V, 504–677); a genuine hurricane (IX, 319–47); and even a dust storm (IX, 445–92). In other words, Lucan's tempests are depicted as epic storms symbolizing the tempestuous spirit of the participators of this Roman drama, particularly, of course, Caesar's. Lucan commanded a special storm technique. He could rely on Virgil and Ovid, but he could also speculate on meteorology and knew his Aratos,[36] and he played on the Stoics' doctrine and fear of the final world flood drowning all creation. Lucan was well versed in the language of the sailors and their art. He uses pathos, intensifies horrors of all kind (e.g., one hand cut off by oars searching for the severed arm), and condenses his hexameters into epigrammatic shortness, particularly in his marine similes.[37]

Grotius must have been interested in the poetic interplay of fortune and fate, in Caesar's ridicule of fate, for fortune operates on his side all the time until the Ides of March, when he is murdered, most likely the climax of a projected Book XII. But Grotius must also have been taken by Lucan's correcting the fortunes of Caesar by a voice of conscience, the ambitious morality of Cato which is bestowed with all the sententiousness the poet can muster. Thus Caesar's moral adversary Cato drums up support for Pompey's side, and Brutus is blended out entirely from the epic as far as it is known.[38] "For if the victor [Caesar] had the Gods on his side, the vanquished ones [Pompey's faction] had their Cato" (I,

128). Perhaps it appealed to Grotius also that Caesar, energy incarnate, acting as an elementary force above the law, found a stoically inclined adversary in Cato, a true *pater patrias* figure.

Generally speaking, Grotius must have felt an affinity toward Lucan's manneristic technique of depicting military features. "Even in subsequent Ages . . . this story of battling will be read . . . and will excite hope enmeshed with fear, and awake useless prayers . . . and one will read about this tragedy, as if it belonged to the future rather than the past. And all readers will still take sides with you, o great Pompey" *(Magnus)*.[39] In other words, the telescoping of time levels interested Grotius the dramatist (as we saw) and also appealed to him as historiographer, (as we shall see). The *Civil War* taught Grotius (and teaches us, the modern reader) how closely, in terms of genre, historic epic and epigrammatic novel are related, whenever a truly tragic subject is treated. Significantly, the traditional gods have no place in such a description. The Fiscal Advocate of Rotterdam devoted his precious spare time to editing critically a baroque civil-war epic of tragic proportions (during the historic truce between Spain and the Netherlands) while he penned the "Remonstrance" and the *Decretum Ordinum* for the Tolerance party. His politics, as his enemies charged in 1618–19, led to the brink of civil war, and certainly to civil strife, in the Netherlands. In this situation, Maurits saw no way other than to stop it from breaking out and arrest the editor of *Civil War*. The classic scholar Grotius could appreciate in literature the depiction of self-destruction. He was well nigh blind to forces bringing about his own fall even when the abyss opened in front of his eyes.

Lipsius's *Germania* edition by Tacitus: Annotations. In the seventeenth century, as far as the subject of politics is concerned, the Roman historian Tacitus replaces the Greek philosopher Aristotle as an authoritative philosopher of empirical methods in describing ruling men in their actions. Tacitus's historical work had already been edited twelve times in the sixteenth century.[40] Between 1574 and 1607 J. Lipsius (1547–1606), the maverick professor of history and law at Leiden University (from 1578–91) edited works by Tacitus in Antwerp and Leiden seven times. Tacitus's famous *Annals and Histories* were taught as college subjects at the University of Leiden and elsewhere in Europe. The Tacitean adaptation became a fashion of imitation,[41] and almost a cult of the educated, particularly in seventeenth-century Netherlands, fighting for independence. Tacitus in the fourth and brilliant book of his *Histories* dramatically narrates the revolt of the Batavians, the ethnical forefathers of the Hollanders. The resistance of the uprising chief, Julius Civilis, against the Romans, and the subsequent arrangement of the insurgent Batavian side with the losing Romans, seemed to convey the glory of statesmanship on the political wisdom of avoiding a cultural separation from the Roman Commonwealth.[42] In the intensity of Holland's battle against Spain, Tacitus's views of liberty (referred to as *libertas novantiqua,* or "rejuvenated liberty," in college) took hold of the educated public. Maurits van Nassau was heralded as a new Civilis. Once the armistice with Spain was concluded, however (and in force between 1609–21), Grotius and others returned to the traditional interpretation of the Batavian leader Civilis as spokesman for peace with Rome.

In 1612, in the same year Grotius delivered his "Annals and History of the Dutch War of Independence" to the States General,[43] a work we shall consider in Chapter 4, a pictorial Tacitus volume treating the Batavian uprising as a civil war under Civilis, appeared in Antwerp. The thirty-six etchings of great patriotic intensity were by Otto Vaenius. The frontispiece, showing two idealized women, one representing "Rome," the other "Batavia," shaking hands on an island, implies a sort of emblematic sisterhood. Below their feet crouch the awestruck rivergods Tiber with the she-wolf and their twins Romulus and Remus, the Dutch river Meuse, and the drunk German Rhine god lying on his back. Their respective rivers seem to merge peacefully at the shores of the capital. The island engulfs a Roman-Dutch territory. It is important, and indicative of Grotius's special interest, to note that on Vaenius's other etchings Civilis's Batavian entourage is dressed in elegant Burgundian costumes;[44] whereas the *Germani* (the ancient Germans) are pictured as dressed in sheepskins and looking stultified and immobile.[45] Vaenius was a friend of Lipsius, who in turn was a friend of Hugo's father, Janus Grotius.

In the twenty-ninth chapter of Tacitus's *Germania,* at the beginning of the second or special part, a description is given of the most outstanding Germanic tribe living outside *Germania* among the Gallians, and of course these are the Batavian ancestors of the Dutch.

Lipsius had edited all of Tacitus's works by 1585, but already by 1581 he had dedicated his *Annals* edition to the States General as a token of gratitude. In his foreword he exhorts the high significance that Tacitus's thinking had had in the fight for freedom by the rebelling Netherlanders. Aided by his publisher Plantijn, whose Antwerp press had been ransacked during the Spanish Fury in 1583, Lipsius indirectly appealed to the Dutch patriots, by teaching them how to raise the artistic discipline of appreciating history into a political science of interpreting history. Lipsius wanted the dramatic and Stoic qualities of Tacitus, the annalist and historian of Rome, to be admired by the educated Leiden group of leading Dutch citizens as a guidepost for Holland. He succeeded in having him read and admired as redactor of "the theater of contemporary life." But Queen Christina of Sweden also is reported to have read a number of pages of Tacitus daily, in order to inspire her to be a capable monarch.[46]

By adding his own annotations to Lipsius's Tacitus edition of 1634 in his 1640 publication, Grotius could express both his appreciation for a brilliant and revered Leiden professor and ingratiate himself to his own Swedish monarch. He was mainly interested in Tacitus's terse "Attic" style, which he could imitate to perfection in Latin, and the literary connection between eloquence and thirst for liberty, the incorruptible, almost Stoic, but nevertheless flamboyant style of Tacitus, the Narbonnensic provincial Roman, whom the great French tragedian Racine once dubbed "the greatest painter of antiquity."[47]

Biblical Text

Annotations to the Old Testament. By the spring of 1619, Grotius, in a missive addressed to his judges at the High Court of Dordrecht, writes that he is not a theologian *(hoewel ik geen theologant ben).*[48] During the following two decades, however, beginning at Loevestein and continuing at Paris and Hamburg, and Paris again, he turned into one of Europe's most respected biblical commentators. We could not find any evidence that his *Annotata ad Vetus Testamentum* (Amsterdam, 1644)[49] were put on the Index of Forbidden Books during his lifetime, as quite a few of his other major works were.[50] On the contrary, his *Annotations* were heavily subscribed to by theologians of all factions until the late eighteenth century.[51] This is all the more astonishing if one recognizes that these annotations were originally only written as a critical and exegetical apparatus to the Bible for the author's own benefit.[52] Together with his *Annotations* to the New Testament, which appeared between 1641 and 1650, the Grotian commentary on the Bible of 4,000 pages in quarto clearly constitutes his *opus magnum (levenswerk).*[53]

This great compendium is not, strictly speaking, a perpetual (running) commentary. Upon checking the editions available to us abroad[54] it turned out, however, that no single book of either Testament, nor the Apocrypha, is left out. Grotius is most fully interested in the major prophets (THE WRITINGS), the Five books of Moses (THE LAW or TORAH), the PSALMS (encompassing the poetic book par excellence of the Old Testament), some of which (51, 88, 114, 130, 137) he had translated in 1600–1601. Concerning the Apocryphal writing, so called after the existing doubt as to their canonicity, he devoted his largest efforts to Ecclesiasticus, a dialectic treatise on wisdom by Jesus son of Sirach, and on the book of Macabees, I–III,[55] a kind of "pathetical writing on history" which had a special appeal for the fan of Lucanus that Grotius was.

Fundamentally, Grotius approaches the Old Testament as the Law imposed by God upon the Hebrews, and hence not, in the first instance, on the Christians. All that could be said with certainty, he thought, was that natural law and Mosaic law were not at odds, albeit that they were neither one and the same.[56] Grotius, in other words, interprets and comments upon Scripture as a historically trained philologist.[57] His interest focuses on textual criticism. Since he does not have access to the oldest manuscripts, he parallelizes similar sayings by Greek and other philosophers, sages, dramatists, or legal writers from all ages in order to verify at least the ethical direction of a particular religious statement in verse or prose. Therefore, by and large, his method of annotating is eclectic and comparative, not unlike the approach he pursues in *Law of War and Peace.* The reader must not be surprised to find cross-references in the *Annotations* to his own juridical masterwork, completed much earlier (1625).

His general point of orientation (and the mark of truth adduced by him) is the use of rationalism rather than an authoritative appeal to mere belief in the supernatural.[58] The writers of the Old Testament, Grotius is convinced, can be trusted, since they were filled with inspiration rather than with zeal merely to propagate faith alone. The mostly anonymous redactors of the Old Testament did not *have* to transmit their Books. They performed their task to uphold or clarify a certain tradition. Wherever Grotius could find attestations to the veracity of biblical sayings, even in unwritten law,[59] he would use them to make a point. Accordingly, Grotius adheres to the principle that a commentator is supposed to avoid all interpretation which is at odds with scriptural tradition.[60] Thus he tries to steer a middle course between rationalism and traditionalism, amalgamating these two roads toward textual explication with great tact. His aim is always to point to the superiority of biblical over profane scripture.[61]

It is fundamental to recognize that Grotius as annotator dropped the scholastics' fourfold method of textual explication[62] and replaced it with a grammatical sense orientation, based on historically verifiable material. Henceforth the Old Testament is treated by this annotator as a spiritual forerunner of and linguistic antecedent to the New Testament, subject to intellectualized criticism. Van Eysinga, however, risks misinterpretation by labeling de Groot's attitude toward the Bible as annotating merely "a piece of World Literature."[63] Grotius does *not* secularize the Bible; rather he tries, often desperately, to save the mystical intellect (or intellectual mysticism) of scriptural material under discussion. He does not anywhere we know of deny the fundamentally necessary belief in Christian miracles as they are recounted in the New Testament or the prophetical commands as given in the Old Testament. In the final analysis, he wants to deduce the "more sublime sense."[64] But, on the other hand, he does not clarify or interpret passages from the Old Testament written in Hebrew for Hebrews, by superimposing on them the authority of the New Testament written in Greek for Christians.[65]

Now we must illustrate his approach and method with a few examples. When discussing Genesis 1, he refers to competing myths of terrestrial creations found among the Phoenicians, Indians, Egyptians, and Greeks. He also adds proof that Neoplatonic philosophers proclaim a similar story, too. With respect to the Creation of the sun, Grotius refers to the Greek philosopher Empedocles. When commenting on

Philological Text Editions

darkness (*chaos*), he refers to the Greek mathematician Thales. That the first woman could not have been created from the "rib" (Gen. 2:2) but from some unspecified part of Adam's body, Grotius deduces from Chaldean and Greek parallel myths. When he annotates Genesis 11:7 ff., the story of the Tower of Babel, he argues that the primeval language could not have been literally the Hebrew of Moses. He shows, instead, that Moses was a linguistic and mythical synthesizer, i.e., a translator.[66] Fundamentally Grotius interprets the Old Testament law as prototype of the Greco-Roman Law. These examples make it clear that Grotius reads the Old Testament scriptures as a dynamic forerunner of several (including legal) developments, and not only in respect to the New Testament. In annotating Leviticus 18:30 ("So keep my charge . . ."[67]) he explains "customs" as incorporating natural law, which in turn is part of God's law.[68] In his introduction to the Psalms their authorship is attributed both to David and to Ezra. In commenting upon these matters (as in other parts of his *Annotations*) he uses phrases such as "it would be stupid to doubt" this or that point. Thus he considers the Song of Solomon most exquisite poetry (*excellentissimum carmen*).[69] Generally speaking, then, and in closing our discussion of the textual side of Old Testament criticism, we are entitled to say that for Grotius historical explication and verification always take precedence over the typological. Only in the last instance and then most sparingly does Grotius resort to the fourfold scriptural sense of intrabiblical interpretation.[70]

Annotations to the New Testament. In order to understand sacred literature addressing itself perennially to a large section of mankind in the hope of increasing their welfare, one has to identify and recognize a basic distinction. While in legal literature (e.g., Justinian's *Institutions*) "justice" as a concept is presumed to be a constant expression of someone's will, the positive or applicable law is adaptable, and hence changeable, by men.[71] In biblical literature, comparatively speaking, redacted by men, which carries a historical significance, the particular meaning of a chapter or verse must also stay unalterable, while exegetic theology, being but a changeable human discipline, varies from generation to generation or from school to school of thought, and hence has to be argued dialectically.[72] As an annotator of major rank, Grotius, by striking a balance between these two poles, the permanent and the *adiaphora*, takes a particular place in the history of exegetical research.

Grotius is decidedly interested in the permanent (unalterable) aspects of New Testament scholarship, not in the dogmatic subtleties of exegetics. He is, moreover, convinced that human rationality, which to him is spiritual, albeit not containing exhaustive clarity in each and every case, would confirm the basic features of the New Testament from within its own resources, but also from ideals common to all major religions. And therefore it could stand extensive annotations, he thought.

In annotating the New Testament, Grotius follows several editorial principles, which can only be briefly summarized here: the New Testament contains Christ's will confirmed by his physical death and resurrection. The Covenant is largely revelational and hence self-explanatory to a certain degree. Grotius only comments when he has something to state or can contribute to a possible solution. The solution may be of his own reasoning or from outside religious or philosophical reading. He always focuses on particular expressions and solves textual problems. When he has decided on a stand, he attempts to avoid deepening the strife between the two confessions in his explanation. He never denies the unity of the New Testament. He does not appeal to God as judge, but to Him as regent,[73] almost an arbiter, who wills the Law.[74] Grotius unequivocally recognizes and accepts the dual nature of Jesus as God and Man; but he scrupulously refrains from getting entangled in disputations about what these two personal elements in Christ are made of in particular.[75]

In his *Annotations* he continually focuses on Christ's works, deeds, and teachings as guideposts for Christians how to act virtuously. Although Christ's deeds challenge Christians, they demand discipleship and reconciliation. Any layman can understand these commands. Grotius also refrains from speculations about the essence of the Holy Spirit.

Having said this, we have to relate now that, as annotator, Grotius clearly prefers certain books over others for his annotations. To the gospel of Matthew he devotes more than one-fifth of his whole annotations, or 580 pages! First of all, he presents this gospel as a manual of Christ's teachings. Next he successively comments on the five major

Philological Text Editions

discourses of Jesus, and on specific themes in chapters 5 to 7, the Sermon on the Mount.[76]

Now let us illustrate some of his specific annotations, e.g., to the beginning of Matthew. He writes that the gospel, properly speaking, does not begin until chapter 4, but that chapters 1–3 form a preface. Matthew, in speaking of Jesus' "disciples" in 5:5, does not refer to the inner circle of the twelve, but rather addresses all those who embrace his teachings. Grotius then proceeds to explain the addition "in spirit" in the Beatitudes (5:3) and refers to Luke 6. The annotator does not think it necessary that the "you" in 5:13 has to refer to the twelve, but again might address the audience listening on the Mount.[77] Grotius then comments on 5:21–48 as illustrations of the true understanding of the Law of God and of righteousness.[78]

The commandment not to swear falsely (5:33 ff.) is not to be construed by man as meaning never to confirm any pledge by an oath (vv. 34–35) as Grotius had shown in *DJBP* II,13,21. To illustrate his method of exegesis with one more example he reminds the pious reader of the New Testament that the words "for thine is the kingdom and the power and the glory, for ever" (6:13) are not contained in the oldest Greek manuscripts, but only in the later Syrian and Latin ones, and that they therefore cannot be attributed to Christ himself.[79]

It is thus our considered opinion that some of Grotius's conjectures have become commonplace in biblical exegesis. My own remarks, and the few pages by Drs. Haentjens and Knight, are not sufficient for a complete summarization. Dr. Kümmel claims that one really could group Grotius together with Martin Luther and J. Camerarius under the heading of "prehistory" of modern exegesis, and then speak of English theism as having given the "decisive new germinal thinking." At least three outstanding seventeenth-century English theologians are openly dependent on and supportive of Grotius's annotative method: Henry Hammond, Thomas Pierce, and William White (= Guilielmus Phalerius).[80] Had it not been for the most ardent and sustained attacks on Grotius by his grand adversary at Wittenberg, the Lutheran theologist Abraham Calovius (1612–1686),[81] Lutheran-Protestant New and Old Testament research in German would have blossomed more fully in the seventeenth, rather than belatedly in the eighteenth, century.[82]

It is not clear yet in which specific respects Grotius erred in his basic assumptions, e.g., in presupposing with Erasmus that Mark extensively used the gospel of Matthew; and that the traditional ending of Mark 16:5–20 "Go into all the World, and preach the gospel . . ." is not inauthentic; in denying that the gospel of Luke was written earlier than that of Matthew and Mark; and in assuming that the gospel of John was written toward the end of the first century A.D. (accepted by the majority of scholars today). In judging the philological merits of both of Grotius's *Annotations* one would have to know and compare the number of sources available or nonavailable to the exiled scholar. The commentating of Holy Scripture (nowadays usually undertaken by one scholar per book) in its entirety by Grotius changed scriptural exegesis, according to E. Hirsch,[83] at least in two major respects: It deemphasized permanently overlabored dogmatic notions, and started to "demythologize" the text, to use a modern term. Second, the question of which parts belong to the canon of Scripture, and which ones may be less than authentic, is separated for good from the issue of how much inspiration went into a particular textual passage. The inclusion of a saying attributed to Jesus or to one of his disciples had henceforth to be argued through logically and historically. In other words, Grotius systematically demonstrates on the basis of deep faith and superior knowledge that the Bible is infallible in most, but not in every, respect. His decades-long work confirmed his belief drawn from thousands of annotations that the New Testament contained by far the oldest and most sacred teachings and the reconstructed history of the Christian religion. This was perhaps a much more fundamental work for the whole of Christianity than the literary pretensions undertaken by Pope Urban VIII, who reigned at the same time (1623–44) and who paraphrased parts of both Testaments into Horatian metrical schemes.[84] Grotius at least bequeathed to every Christian reader of the Bible that not the canon but the miraculous revelations, properly understood, contained the essence and foundation[85] of the church eternal. In any event, he wrote his *Annotations* to the Bible in the expectation and the well-founded hope that they might be of profit for readers of future generations.[86]

Chapter Four
Scholarly Study of Patriotic History

His Native Country Holland

States' Parallels of Ancient and Modern Times. Shortly after Grotius was employed as Latin Historiographer of Holland and West Friesland in 1601,[1] he embarked upon his source study of ancient Dutch patriotic history. Scholars agree that the year of 1601–2 is the most likely period during which the *Parallelon Rerumpublicarum* were written.[2] An adequate paraphrase of the Latin title would be "On the Customs and Native Genius of the Athenians, Romans, and Batavians: A comparison of Statehood."[3]

The *States' Parallels* have the character of a preliminary[4] study still in draft form; they were not meant for publication, but were discovered among Grotius's papers. The first and second books are said to be "lost," but we shall see that the latter one grew into a more mature literary form after all. The third book contains twenty-six chapters and represents medium-sized essays on ethical comparisons which could be deduced as clichés when one compared Batavian or Old-Hollandic customs and their character, on the one hand, to Greco-Roman ones on the other. The essayist tags himself a "Batavian," and this betrays his bias. Only the first two chapters of the manuscript deal with these three peoples ethnologically. Chapters 3–10 compare ethical with unethical political practices in history; 11–17 deal with domestic Hollandic issues—food, intoxication, sobriety, etc.; 18–19 return to Lipsian-Ciceronian considerations about "constancy," "inborn genius," and political "prudence." The end, chapters 20–26, treat loosely grouped topics of comparative patriotic interest. Although at first sight the total structural organization is not quite cogent,[5] four interrelated themes, brought up in Chapter 1, are alluded to in almost all subsequent chapters, namely *gens, corpus, mos, ingenium* (= populace, physical features, moral customs, and "national" characteristics or, rather, prejudices), and are given comparisons tilted in favor of the Hollanders.

It seems possible, though, to speak of a sort of outline in respect to all but the last chapters. One could make it read as follows: 1–2, ethnological comparisons; 3–7, juridical matters; 8–11, moral values; 12–17, historical parallels; 18–19, ethical customs; 20–21, military and naval matters; 22–26, cultural-historical excursuses.[6] One could, therefore, with some justification recognize in Grotius's statehood parallelisms an open filing cabinet, in which the collector recasts his knowledge he had gathered from his private reading and the experience which he had accrued by acting in the public arena. By this arrangement Grotius intended to distill information from the lessons of ancient history for the benefit of his contemporaries, the Netherlanders then being called "Belgians." In other words, we look into a direct forerunner of political science in the form of patriotic histories moralisées. The nucleus of this subject was already being taught at the University of Leiden at the turn of the century. It is meant to serve as a practical philosophy of political neostoicism.[7] The third book of the *States' Parallels* tries to prove and establish that in respect to liberty the Romans and Greeks were not superior. Grotius wants his readers to be convinced that the natural Hollandic genius which rose spontaneously in the ancient past[8] was not inferior to that of the classical city states of Athens and Rome at all. He researches by means of a shuttle technique back and forth from ancient history to modern times, thus making "Batavian patriotic time" reversible in direction.[9] In most general terms, he declares Holland "the sworn enemy of bad faith and tyranny" from Roman time onwards to his present. In this light we shall proceed to illustrate Grotius's comparative method and comment on the following outstanding chapters, 6, 21, 24, 25, and 26, which we consider pivotal for the interpretation of the future writing of Hugo Grotius. Fikentscher calls Grotius's "historical method," pursued in Parallelon III, and particularly the sixth chapter, good versus bad faith, "naively antiquarian"[10] in the dogmatic sense of his *Methoden des Rechts*.[11] In 1601 the young advocate describes the genre of his *Parallelon* at the end of his *Sacra in quibus* in different terms: "A comparison between our Republic and other formerly renowned ones as well as their successes will have a bearing on [the discipline of] political science" *(scientia civilis).*[12]

Grotius, in his Chapter 6, sets out to prove by political means that good faith as a trait is abundantly prevalent among the ancient and present Hollanders. His line of argument is made unequivocal from the start: he looks for corroboration everywhere, e.g., by praising Maurits for not having used the time-honored but despicable methods of poisoning cisterns (such as the unfaithful Athenians did) while the fortress Grol was unfaithfully held by the Spanish. The other main point is that the Batavians were superior in keeping the political good faith in comparison to other obviously less reliable Germanic tribes from the times of Caesar on to Grotius's own time, e.g., in the fight against the Spaniards. In short, he wishes to establish that "politically faithful" and "Batavian" are synonymous terms. Therefore, he coins the term "Batavian good faith" as a springboard for a study he is working on simultaneously, *De Antiquitate Reipublicae Batavicae,*[13] and contrasts it with "Spanish bad faith" oppressing Dutchmen with *punica crudelitas.* Grotius goes a decisive step further than his predecessor, Simon Stevin, in *Vita Politica: Het Burgherlick leven* (Leiden, 1590), who had named Athens and Rome and Switzerland as guideposts for identifying the Batavian character of the Republic he was describing and defending.[14] The Batavian arch-virtue of "good faith" becomes even more outstanding in Grotius's description when contrasted to the vices of the Dutchmen's enemies. The German Emperor does not hesitate to levy troops against the Republic in Flanders and Utrecht, when he should have defended her instead. "Even Holland herself was given away," sighs the political recorder. In any case, the vices of the Spaniards surpass even those of the infidel Turks, whereas the Batavians are the only ones who did not ever perform a breach of confederation *(foedifragus);* even against heretics one has to keep good faith, insists Grotius. Toward the end of this chapter he reverts to "standard Roman cruelty" committed against the Batavians, then condescendingly called Barbarians, a stain on their honor, which even Tacitus could not whitewash. This painting in black and white is kept up by our 'advocate from Holland' until the end of his whole diatribe.[15]

Quite apart from the characteristics of the three principal peoples treated in this tract, an axiomatic link is being established between good faith and search for freedom: "Let the whole world recognize that to stand in the breach for freedom, and to stand in the breach for good faith flows from the same moral source." Here Grotius found the key theme to his future scholarly study of patriotic history.[16] A comparison dealing with fisheries, merchant-marine traffic, and navigation is found in Chapter 21, *"De Re Maritima."* The Dutch herring is addressed as "king of the fish." The Dutch navy is heroic and decent in its superior art of seafaring. It counts among its ranks the seamen who command the winning tactics in battles. Their enemies are no better than unworthy pirates. Tell me the corners of the sea to which Dutch seamen have not sailed! Which other heavily populated country besides Holland possesses as many ships as houses, huts not excluded from the count? Where else can more than a thousand ships, at 1,500 guilders apiece, be built during one single year? Where else does every little village harbor nautical experts, astronomers, hydrographers, etc.?

In Chapter 24, entitled "On Many Kinds of Erudition," de Groot sings the praise of Desiderius Erasmus[17] by speaking directly to his ancestor-in-spirit: "O Erasmus, greatest of Batavian virtues, how can words be impressive enough to describe your singular erudition, your celestial genius, your incomparable diligence?" And then Grotius elevates the sage from Rotterdam into the sphere of the numinous, and declares him to have become the possession of the whole world. This exceptional praise is paralleled by Grotius's raising of Holland as a paragon of "a more educated humanity" *(Hollandia . . . locus politiori humanitati).*[18] Grotius, who just heralded Erasmus as the "father of Letters" in the last chapter, now addresses the subject of language in Chapter 25, *"De Lingua."* Being a member of the republic of letters himself (except that he did not seem to have known English) he addresses himself to the problems of efficiency of languages, particularly Greek, Latin, and Dutch, relative to each other. He voices his conviction that the nation to be held the wisest is the one that thought out the most efficient and effortless system of communication.[19] The pronunciation of a language such as Dutch internalizes some of the customs practiced in civil life. Less than distinct pronunciation betrays traces of barbarity. Athenian Greek is graced "with a masculine sound." The Roman language gradually changed with changing customs from "rough" to "delicate" *(sic).* High German sounds "harder," Dutch "softer," which latter, in respect to richness of expression, is without equal—states the "public relations counselor."[20] Grotius, in order to influence the Dutch to think highly of their own linguistic sophistication, voices regret that Dutch instruction to outlanders has not been made as attractive as French instruction to foreigners. Of late the absurdity has spread that native speakers of Dutch have to feel exiles in their own language and country by aping foreign tongues. Stevin, however, did the right thing in praising the suitability of Dutch for treating mathematics, chemistry, and military science,[21] subjects taught at the University of Leiden.

Grotius's observations on the abundance of root words *(primigeniis vocabulis)* go back directly to Stevin.[22] In the main part, de Groot makes many pertinent comments on rudimentary comparative linguistics, a subject for a separate dissertation. Stated briefly, he reflects on sign, sound and meaning, root words, Gallic borrowing, and Crimean Gothic, and develops an embryonic loanword hypothesis. He stresses the exemplary character of what we now call Old Germanic, and antedates Zipf's principle of least effort in languages: *Ita linguae laus prima censenda est, exprimere quam minimo mentem,*[23] and continues: what is of greater value than to express many things by as few signs as possible, in which process effort and time are being saved? New words are constantly being generated and are understandable just as well as hereditary ones.[24] With us there are just as many words available as there are thoughts expressible—reminding one of the argument that there are just as many ships as there are houses in Holland.

In the final chapter, 26, *"De religione et Pietate,"* he sings the praise of Calvinist free conscience and tolerance, and argues in favor of an unrestricted practical piety. His attitude betrays the influence of Franciscus Junius (= Du Jon), professor of theology at Leiden, and his *Eirenicon* (Leiden, 1593), as well as Dirck Volkertzoon Coornhert.[25] It is important to recognize that *pietas* in the field of practical devotion takes the same place in Grotius's final arguments as "good faith" did in Chapter 6 of his *Parallels*. As good faith leads to freedom from foreign domination, truly Christian piety leads to the inner freedom of conscience. Proudly Grotius intonates: we have rubbed off the greenspan which grew on top of true religion for many a century! Let each and every one of us believe what he can, and hold his own devotional service *(godsdienst)*! Holland's genius and intelligence are daily on the rise! With this jubilant confession ends the third book of the *States' Parallels*.

Ancient Holland and Its Sovereignty. Grotius published his *De antiquitate Reipublicae Batavicae* in 1610, but mentions his booklet as essentially finished in his *States' Parallels* by 1601–2. He even asks the reader to check the evidence for the propositions there himself. We rather doubt whether *Ancient Holland* was much revised during the intermittent years. In the foreword, Grotius at first seems to joke about his method of presentation. There the booklet is said "to write itself." But actually he is serious, and defines his rules of historical evidence as "marshaled facts" which are "counseled by reason, approved by experience, and recommended by antiquity."[26] The work presents a "States' Parallel," too, or rather, an inquiry into the state of the States' Parallels that exist between ancient Batavia and modern seventeenth-century Holland. At the end of Chapter 1 he admonishes himself: the state historian ought to proceed as arbitrator, but he should not "too curiously or too precisely urge testimony" (approximately: press his facts too hard) "from every moment of time to the next."

Since the beginning, i.e., the point of republican statehood called "principality" *(principatus),* is known, according to Grotius, and the end points back toward that beginning, all the chronicler has to do is to fill in the missing links, the building blocks of past histories. But the very term he uses for the beginnings, "antiquity," is a rather exploited one. For the point of departure is legendary only, and does not, as charged, "successively develop" toward Hollandic statehood. The building blocks he assembles are not interlocking like sap trenches in a fortification system. The missing parts are bridged and glossed over by moral and patriotic considerations. Grotius shows how the three principal state building factors which are said to be piety *(religio),* equity *(justitia),* and unity *(concordia)* interlock in chapters 1–7. Chapter 1 tries to establish that the government by principality, as distinct from monarchy, can lead just as safely to the formation of statehood by *ordines* of the leading figures, as kingships can. In Chapter 2 he traces the interplay of these factors through the histories of the beginning of the Batavian people *(condita gente,* in obvious allusion to the Latin historian Livy's *Ab urbe condita).* Thus already by Chapter 2 the Old Batavian Commonwealth *(respublica)* becomes the prototype of seventeenth-century Holland.[27] In Chapter 3 the State of the Old Batavians survives

Scholarly Study of Patriotic History

the time of the Roman monarchy (first century A.D.). Julius Civilis appears again, only this time to address "Gallos" (Wallons) and Batavos (Hollanders) with patriotic speeches, telling the latter tribe that they are free from Roman tributes. His principal source is still Tacitus and his three main works, *Historiae, Germania,* and *Annales,* which are invoked far too often to sound convincing, not to speak of mere persuasion by circumstantial evidence. In fact, many classical writers are quoted in order to fill in the missing facts, rather than have the sources speak for themselves. In Chapter 4 the state of the Batavian Commonwealth during the epoch of the fall of the Roman Empire (the third and fourth centuries A.D.) is examined. Grotius invents "an increase in the Batavian valor," but must admit that "all the rest is very obscure." It is then shown how, during the fifth century, Holland became an earldom *(comitatus),* in which the basic liberty was not infringed upon. Again and again the young statographer points to an assumed succession of Old Batavian sovereignty, coupled with ancient liberty, for the purpose of cementing a foundation of legitimacy for the State of Holland: liberty won overpowers the tyranny of terror; liberty upheld throughout centuries gives rise to fidelity among the citizens. The state founded upon that ideal comes close to the ideal state which Plato had in mind.[28] The high point of Chapter 5 is reached when Grotius narrates the temporary decrease of liberty incurred by the Great Privileges of Holland and Zeeland decreed by Mary of Burgundy in 1477.[29] From there he takes a giant step toward the chronicling of his own time. He obviously intends to prove over and over that the County of Holland, freighted by so many laws, has not enjoyed the right of sovereign power completely. The sixth chapter vividly depicts tyrannical abuses of power as stimulants to wars which lead to justified rebellions. All of a sudden he reverts to the Carolingian period, only to jump forward again into the War of Independence in the latter part of the sixteenth century, so that one could say that the seventh and final chapter is a draft for the beginning of his subsequent book, *Annales et Historiae.* This study of his was partially finished in a form unknown to us by 1612.[30] The copy which he presented to the States of Holland at that time must be considered lost.

Grotius pursues only two aims in his pragmatic study of the patriotic history of Holland: tendentiously, a continuous linking of the elements of power in a chain of succession is sought. For if it did not snap or break, Holland-Batavia never completely lost governmental self-rule as a republic;[31] and hence, second, Holland was entitled to the perpetual restitution of ancient independence. This argument also plays a role in the famous *apologeticus,* written on behalf of the lawful government of Holland against accusers at The Hague and Dordrecht, in 1622.[32] There, as here, Grotius argues for the benevolent rule of the state by aristocrats, based on the law of status, but not resting on the sovereignty of the people.[33]

In summarizing, we must admit that *Ancient Holland* in all probability constitutes one of the least scientific writings of Grotius. It is true that he formed and sharpened his historical judgment and that he followed to a point J. J. Scaliger's *Opus de emendatione temporum* (1583). On the other hand, he deliberately falls below the level of historicity attained by Jean Bodin (1530–1596),[34] where in Chapter 4 the *delectus,* the choice between variably accurate sources, is recommended as the historian's only scientific method of obtaining reliability. Grotius seems simply to have ignored this advice. This is a puzzle, since he does allude to Bodin in his notes attached to his edition. Surprisingly the standard modern *Handboek tot de staatkundige Geschiedenis der Nederlanden,*[35] surveying the development of the Netherlands from the beginning up to 1555, ignores the work of Grotius, researched as patriotic history achieved by Holland, the chief state within the Union.

Annals and Histories of the Dutch War of Independence. On his death-bed, Grotius predicted that of all of his writings, his *Annals and Histories* deserved to make him immortal as a writer;[36] for on and off he had worked on its arrangement, contents, and style from 1601–43, during all of his productive years. In other words, he was confident that his literary executors, his brother Willem and the Vossius family, would see the eventual publication through and that the response of the public would be very favorable. In this regard, however, he had underestimated his middle son, Pieter, who brought the book out ten years after his father's death, and had overestimated the appeal of his work to the public. Why was Grotius so very attached to this particular work? Was he worried that his reputation would spread through the international republic of letters, but not be sufficiently recognized in Holland? In any case, he seems to have expressed the hope that his fame as a scholar would not stay separated from his native

Dutchness indefinitely after his death. Or, to put it in another way, he died hoping to the last moment that his political exile would not turn into a literary banishment from his native and beloved Holland.

After he had finished his first draft and circulated it among amicable persons, he wrote to his old friend Daniel Heinsius, who had just been promoted to full professor of history at Leiden, in 1613: "It gives me a tremendous satisfaction to reenter the marvellously laid out traces of our antiquity, during which historical period one lived more wholesomely [*sanctius*] than we live today."[37] Grotius felt a more intimate relation to this, his historical, main work than to his professional occupation. The former covered the discipline of patriotic history, which he tried to record. He had been appointed Latin historiographer of the States of Holland and Westfriesland at the behest of his mentor, Oldenbarnevelt, with an official charge to write the Low Countries' wars of independence. He chose to write it from shortly before the beginning (1559) to the Twelve-Year truce with Spain in 1609.

In October 1612, he submitted a version to Holland's Committee of Counsellors, which must have been passed around among leading experts. Ter Meulen-Diermanse and Kampinga, considering evidence after such a long lapse of time, leave it open whether this manuscript, now lost, was in publishable form or not. Apparently the committee did not think so for unknown, but most likely political, reasons and ruses. Already in 1613 Grotius had been proposed as a federal deputy member to the States General. As late as 1614, Barnevelt is known to have read this manuscript himself. Significantly we gather this information from a letter of Grotius to Heinsius.[38] In a letter to the French historian of highest standing, J. A. de Thou (= Thuanus), Grotius makes a revealing confession: "I *wove* [*pertexui*] the history of our war to the end, that is, until the year of the truce [1609].[39] Now the labor of checking and correcting is left, which is almost more cumbersome than the actual writing."[40] In other words, by 1615, the writer himself knew that this oeuvre was *not* in publishable form. Since the States of Holland and Westfriesland had commissioned this work for pay, it is fair to assume that the approved edition would have been one dedicated to the sponsor. There was, however, a serious political problem. Grotius chose as his opening phrase that he set out to describe "the most famous war of our times, which may, not improperly, be called confederate [*sociale*]

. . ."—a loaded term which contains a program in itself. For it describes in a nutshell Grotius's theory of independent States' power, and of feudally based independence of the several states from a central government joined as the "Burgundian Circle" in the Treaty of Augsburg (1548) and reaffirmed by the Union of Utrecht in 1579, with respect to Spain, as well as the Holy Roman Empire of the German Nation.[41] Holland's government had paid the lion's share of financing this all-Dutch war of independence. Accordingly, it expected his historiographer to do his duty and give that lion's share proper recognition in respect to the leading role Holland wished to have played even in the far-distant past. Therefore, it is no coincidence that Grotius's *Ancient Holland* (which internally must be thought of as *States' Parallels, Book II*[42]) is a prelude *(voorstudie)* to this main work. In our opinion, the confederate point of view could be construed as containing the intellectual seeds for the charge leveled against de Groot in the accusations of 1618–19 that he established a state within the state. In order to forestall such an interpretation, Grotius stresses over and over again the military genius and the superior campaign techniques of the federal head, Maurits. To us, at least, it is unthinkable that the draft, on which Grotius had worked eleven years, was not accepted because of presentational deficiencies.

While the 1615 publication of the *Annals and Histories* was still a pending issue not to be resolved, an engraving was printed and circulated which showed the thirty-two-year-old, but actually very young and vigorous-looking, syndicus (city governor) of Rotterdam (see frontispiece), anonymously engraved after J. van Ravesteyn, with an epigram by Daniel Heinsius, dated 1614. This sharply pointing epigram, an answer to Grotius's last passaic ode to his own birthday in 1614, is the last known pro-Grotian poem from the pen of his old *halsvriendt*,[43] incidentally from the year in which the regular correspondence between them ends also:

> *Depositum caeli, quod iure Batavia mater*
> *Horret, et haud credit se peperisse sibi*
> *Talem oculis, talem ore tulit se maximus Hugo.*
> *Instar crede hominis, caetera crede Dei.*

(The very remarkable HUGO here presents himself, according to his likeness, to the viewer, as a trustee of heavens, about whom Mother Batavia is rightly terrified, not believing that she gave birth to him by herself. Believe me, it is the portrait of a man, but trust also, that it is in the image of God!)[44]

Heinsius's expression "trust/trustee of the heavens" poetically weaves *syndicus* (written on the oval surrounding the picture) and *cura* (lines 14 and 36 of his thirty-first birthday poem) and the biblical image of *depositum custodi* (truth entrusted to the trustee) and the idea of treasures in heaven, together.[45] The theological basis of this special depositing act is *fides* ("faith"). As is the case with Grotius's birthday ode, this epigram returns with its last word to the opening word (*instar . . . dei* to *depositum caeli*), whereby "the image of God" can be used by medieval Latin-writing commentators for *in imaginem dei* ("in the Image of God"[46]) as an expression for Adam. Since Heinsius collaborated with Grotius on the publication of *Adamus Exul,* it is fair to state that the epigram reviews the total Grotius up to 1614, as he presented himself in the eyes of "Mother Batavia," i.e., the educated public of Holland. So it is only at first sight (and for the public at large) that the professional historian from Leiden University seems to eulogize the greatest Grotius, the political custodian of Batavian history and liberty, and church governance for that matter, out of all proportions. We do not hesitate to surmise that he must have read the manuscript of *Annales et Historiae* before he wrote this epigram, just as he had read the manuscript of Grotius's *Ancient Batavia* four years earlier.[47] The insider—but perhaps not the addressee himself?—could not have overheard the stern public warning that Old Holland was shuddering at her own son, having reached the zenith of his rise in her service. Does this warning even foreshadow the image of Timothy (Grotius), heir apparent to Paulus (Barnevelt)? Probably not! In any case, we must marvel at the extraordinary perception of Daniel's poetic imagery. For as of 1615–18, Grotius's fall from that pinnacle was picking up momentum, which made the publication of an officially sponsored history of the republic politically less and less feasible, and finally impossible, in Grotius's lifetime. Even posthumously, the States of Holland and Westfriesland did not agree to the publication. Mother Batavia, so to speak, has never stopped shuddering since.

In 1625, the Parisian exile de Groot admits to his friend Vossius that he could not publish his *Annals* as yet; in 1628 again he confesses to Vossius that he had better recheck on other sources.[48] After he realized that the state of affairs in the Netherlands during the 1630s made the appearance impossible, he proposes to his superior, Swedish Chancellor Count Axel Oxenstierna, whether he could not dedicate his *Annals and Histories*, "which are in shape to be published with benefit" to Her Majesty, Queen Christina of Sweden.[49] This request, apparently, was not granted. Finally, the manuscript arrived in Holland in 1638 and was handed to the respected publisher Blaeuw—again to no avail. The aging author then started revising again, and in January 1645 the printing began in earnest. Grotius's death, occurring half a year later, slowed down the process, so that his oeuvre did not see the light of day until 1657, and then, valid for fifteen years, ironically, by Imperial German Privilege. Although the States General joined, the states of Holland and Westfriesland still took exception.[50] In fairness to Grotius, this short genesis of the book he considered his main work was necessary.

Now we shall discuss the structure of the *Annals and Histories*. It cannot be understood without immediate reference to Grotius's chosen model, Tacitus's *Historiae* and *Annales*. These *Historiae* encompass four complete and a fifth, fragmented book, covering the reign of the Three and the Flavian Emperors, A.D. 69–96,[51] about twenty-eight years of rule. His *Annals*, on the other hand, written much later, covered the reign of the Julian-Claudian Emperors, A.D. 14–68, originally in eighteen books.[52] By reversing and putting together the traditional Tacitean order of titling, Grotius wished to imply that *his* studies were written from the beginning of the War of Independence, arranged in the chronological order (militarily begun in 1568 and temporarily stopped by the truce of 1609). His first part, the *Annals* (A), are thus arbitrarily given five chapters and encompass about twenty-eight to twenty-nine years, i.e., the events of 1559–88. On the other hand, he gives eighteen chapters to his *Historiae* (H), with a deliberately shortened and fragmented last chapter, so as to stay Tacitean and to intimate that Batavia only achieved a truce, not quite yet a permanent peace, with Spain.[53]

Henri C. A. Muller[54] made a preliminary study of the historiographical sources and came to the conclusion that Grotius did not use documents properly called such until he wrote on his own time in office (1607) in his fourth chapter of H. According to his findings, Grotius by and large used the summaries of Dutch-Latin, Spanish/Italian-Latin, and classical Latin writers. He must have relied heavily on his and his family's and older friends' memories of events. The main Dutch-Latin sources of the first category used are by Pieter Bor (a), E. van Meteren (b), and E. van Reydt (c).[55] A critical edition of the *Annals and Histories* would have to trace many dozens of documents and general sources beyond those few listed by Muller in 1919. Since Grotius spent more time on this work than on any other of his writings, and was always in the habit of assembling as many sources as were available to him,[56] the list may be expected to be large.

Concerning the historiographical method employed, Muller, who up to the present must still be considered an expert on the subject, terms it "pragmatic" in his second chapter. This term, in our opinion, is well chosen; in fact, the one appropriate for describing Grotius's lengthy study of this particular Dutch military or campaign history. It reflects certain outspoken biases which are adhered to by many outstanding military historians. His work and its approach is moralizing; it suggests even to Non-Netherlanders that they can *learn* from this campaign history. The reader is supposed to appreciate the meaning of "liberty," "sovereignty," "virtue," "magnanimity," and "measuredness." Pro-Orangist statements go hand in hand with the author's aristocratic and learned outlook. That the bubonic plague claimed roughly twenty thousand Dutch lives in 1601 is not mentioned, but the death of Lipsius is recorded under the year 1606. There is no doubt in this interpreter's mind that the mature Grotius was still eagerly patriotic and hence very favorably disposed toward the significance of the history of *Belgia*/Netherlands. Grotius probably rewrote this oeuvre so many times because he wanted to shame his critics back home and the cynics in France, and to increase mankind's awareness of a higher vocation in this struggle by the Netherlands. With these points in mind, we now have to decide whether the *Annales et Historiae* are a humanistic work of historical science, in the restricted sense of the usage of the seventeenth century or whether essentially and predominantly they present themselves as a work of art, or are perhaps a bit of both.

We perceived that Grotius's historiography, although less inflammatory than in the *States' Parallels,* and also grown more sophisticated since the days of his *Ancient Holland,* is still not on a par basis with exigencies of the leading historiographical writing of his own times.[57] The whole work is interlaced with many cultural-historical excursions, brilliant admonitions in the envelope of ficticious oratory (which may, however, have some historical basis of fact), and occasional very well executed site or city descriptions.[58] With all these excursions and some invented details, which are not directly related to the main thread, but are called for to keep the danger of annalistic monotony at bay, we adjudge Grotius's descriptive masterpiece a forerunner of subsequent so-called *historian's history*—minus the source studies![59] We must, however, keep in mind that we only try to ascertain an approximation, not an exhaustive historiographical terminology. Grotius's method *is* lacking objectivity, but it intends to catch a panoramic view. This is not to deny, on the other hand, that there are *few* factual errors contained, which Muller lists at the end of his fourth chapter. The argument in favor of terming A and H a work of art[60] hinges on the significance of its form, expressed by Grotius's chosen and brilliantly sustained style, rather than its—admittedly not totally unficticious—contents.

Structurally, as we perceived, Grotius followed the model of Tacitus. Tacitus's *Historiae,* Book IV, containing the revolt of the Batavians, was germinal for the inception of *Ancient Holland,* but plays only a minor role in the beginning of Grotius's *Annals.* Muller wholeheartedly endorses the opinion of preceding scholars, that by and large Grotius's mature historical style ought to be termed "Tacitean." This opinion has been carefully researched by E. L. Etter[61] and has been modified. She demonstrated that our writer shares with Tacitus the partially abrupt shortness and density *(Gedrängtheit)* of his sentence structure. Muller could also establish the particular point that Grotius likes to use adjectival constructions to which a genitive is added (e.g., *ambiguus animi,* "ambiguous of mind"). Much more important, on the other hand, is the fact that one has trouble tracing and verifying typical Tacitean stylistic expressions in the text. And yet there is a direct allusion to Caesar's famous opening phrase, *Gallia est omnis divisa in partes tres* ("All of Gaul is divided into three regions") in *Germania est omnis divisa in pagos decem* ("All of Germany is divided into ten areas").[62] In other words, as a whole, Grotius's mature historical style is neither strongly Tacitean nor overly Caesarean; rather it is mildly Caesarean-Tacitean. He does not use as many remote or archaic words as Tacitus; rather he coins new expressions.[63] Nor does Grotius feature prominently, as Caesar does in his *Gallic War* and his *Commentaries to the Civil War*. Although we would argue that Grotius also attempted to describe and depict histories *sine ira et studio* ("objectively and without bias")[64] we can say no more than that by now he sides less fervently with Mother Batavia than he did in his youth. Clearly, however, what is the honor of Rome for Tacitus is the honor and the fulfillment of the newly formed Netherlands *(Belgia)* for Grotius. He also does not betray a propensity for tragic history in his later historical writing, as Tacitus does in his master work, the *Annales*. Nor does Grotius pose as much a moral judge of customs and vices as Tacitus. He shows some of Tacitus' brevity, but not his frequent terseness bordering on the obscure. Neither does Grotius share here or elsewhere Caesar's proverbial cynicism. Tacitus clearly had a pessimistic, and Grotius a much more optimistic, outlook on history and its recording.

Grotius's mature historical style is referred to by Etter as "Attic."[65] This is a classic style in Greek as well as in Latin marked by simplicity and directness and avoidance of rhetorical adornment. Its opposite model of style is characterized by a fulsomeness both in conception and execution, and is referred to as "Asianic." Both style models are imitatory, and both are used during the so-called Silver Latin period in Rome. The student of literature will realize the difference between these two styles, if he thinks of a flowery Latin doctor's diploma (Asianic style) compared to a terse notification that the candidate fell through his *examen rigorosum* (Attic style). Caesar himself was a stylistic Atticist, and Cicero in his *Orator* sharply anti-Atticistic.[66] In that sense, then, Grotius may be termed an "Atticist" in his *Annales and Historiae*. We would prefer, however, to go one step further, and give Grotius's propensity for Stoicism, which he did not shake off later in his life, as he did the influence of Seneca, more credit than Etter. Therefore, in summarizing we term Grotius's mature historical style Stoic-Attic, or, if allowed, *Stoattic. It is a style perfectly suited for rendering an historical event or an historical character as vivid as can be, e.g., the characterization of the great Spanish opponent, Granvella of Parma, William of Orange, Philipp II of Spain, or Elizabeth I of England. These characterizations on both sides, pro- and anti-Dutch, are undoubtedly written without historical bias. He never reveals anywhere that he had an axe to grind with his former persecutor, Maurits of Nassau, or with Spanish furies in conducting a brutal war of suppression. He calmly records, as a historian should. Perhaps this is the place to record also a technicality, which will make the description of his Attic style clearer. It is a variant of *classical* Latin. The translator of Grotius almost never needs to consult a medieval or middle Latin dictionary, but rather only classical ones, except in the area of law. Grotius writes as well as the best of the classical Roman writers. He was, in other words, a great Latinist, a thoroughly trained classical scholar. No other Dutch-born writer of the first half of the seventeenth century surpasses Grotius in the quality of his erudite Roman Stoattic style. Grotius from 1603–43 was the most outstanding author of the Latin tongue in the Netherlands. His *Annales and Historiae,* even in their posthumous form of appearance, is a masterwork of rare Latin beauty. We feel that both rudimentary scientific description and artistic perspective are present in Grotius's historical main work. His criticism of the phases of the War of Independence is both balanced and sober. His occasional attempts of epicizing events stay in the background.[67] But the artistic elements are ultimately stronger than the chronicler's awareness of all the pertinent sources. His patriotism is the mainspring of describing Dutch military matters in elegant form.

His Adoptive Country Sweden

A Chronicle of the Norsemen (**An Old Scandinavian Reader**). While Grotius acted as Sweden's ambassador to the court of Louis XIII, he incurred problems in the area of diplomatic protocol. Since Sweden had joined the great European powers rather belatedly, when precedence mattered and counted, Grotius on state occasions representing his new country felt that the honor of Sweden was slighted. Consequently, he made up his mind to defend the Swedes' honor with his pen. He set out to describe the splendor of grand old Scandinavian and hence modern Swedish power, as well as "their moral equivalence to the Romans."[68] He informed Oxenstierna of his literary endeavor.[69] He wanted fully to retrace and document the antiquity of the "Ancient Swedish Empire" from the very beginning of the ethnic migrations from Scandinavia to the Continent.

The enormity of this undertaking by one writer suggests that Grotius's plans originated a few years before he informed the Chancellor of them in 1636. In our opinion, his studies reach back to his Hamburg sojourn, 1632–34. We know that he could use there the rather extensive library of his old Leiden friend, the German Fredericus Lindenbrog (Tiliobroga), who lived from 1573–1648 and who professionally edited Germanic Barbaric Laws *(Leges Barbarorum)*. Among these editions was one on Paulus Diaconus, *De Gestis Langobardorum,* published three times,[70] which Grotius perused. By 1637 Oxenstierna agreed in writing that the planned volume could be dedicated to him, for which Grotius had asked permission.[71] The publisher chosen by Grotius and the Vossius family—G. J.'s son Isaac Vossius (1618–89) had joined the venture—was L. Elzevier at Amsterdam. Isaac Vossius was eminently qualified to oversee the publication on the scientific side. For he had helped Professor Franciscus Junius with the latter's edition of Bishop Ulfila's gospels in Gothic. The trouble this time was an *embarras de richesse*. Elzevier's was planning another Prokopius edition besides Grotius's by none other than Daniel Heinsius. Characteristically (and stoically!) Grotius is reported to have been willing to join his old friend in this venture. At least this willingness to cooperate is noticeable in several of Grotius's letters from Paris.[72] But nothing came of it. Grotius's own *Historia Gotthorum, Vandalorum & Langobardorum,* gracing the three principal tribes' names, thought to have been the forebears of the Swedes, appeared shortly after Daniel Heinsius's death in 1655.[73] It was edited by Isaac Vossius, who out of modesty does not name himself in the address to the reader but who undoubtedly put together the in-depth index of almost 100 pages. According to Fockema Andreae,[74] Grotius did not have the chance to put the final touches on his manuscript.[75]

Were it not for the Introduction, (I 1) the additional source (I 2) study, and the Grotian Old Germanic Glossary (III), we would have had to list this "Scandinavian" chronicle under Chapter 3. But this reader does not only contain historical, but also juridical information on old Germanic laws. This study, in our opinion, belongs in the category of political history, a classification absent in Ter Meulen-Diermanse. It would, however, be in the interest of continuity to keep the TMD numbering in future Grotian scholarship, and not to introduce new ones. Grotius's pro-Swedish work aims at providing points of precedence over both English and French pretensions, and hence political arrogance, that was accorded Grotius by British and French governmental staff. It expresses Grotius's neopatriotic attitude as first ambassador of Sweden to the Court of Louis XIII and to Richelieu. Grotius sets out to prove several points, e.g., that the Swedish tribes were of the noblest lineage. Second, he tries to equate *Scandinavia* (Pliny's expression) and *Scandia* (Ptolemy) with *Scandza* (Jordanes) and *Scantia* (Edward the Confessor's expression). It was also to be equated with the Saxon's *Suetia* = *Suedia* = *Sueonia*. These considerations, voiced in Grotius's Introduction, climax in the statement: "These three peoples, Swedes, Norwegians, and Danes [tribes] distributed unequally among them Scandinavia. Their common name is Norsemen [*Nortmanni*], as they are referred to by other European peoples" (10). These remarks are followed by detailed critical studies about the Goths, Gets, Vandals, and Langobards, which have become commonplace in the discussion of this branch of Germanic philology.[76] We need to stress, however, that Grotius, without access to all the ancient sources now available, attempted to put together a chronology of Gothic, Vandalic, and Langobardic kings.[77] The remarks bear the character of glosses and commentaries to the original texts by Germanic historians of the Dark Ages who wrote in Latin. His *elogia* is a short dissertation based on his own translations of Germanic sources written in Greek into Latin, as far as they were available to him in Paris.

Grotius's collection and glossary of what are now called East Germanic words were of outstanding importance for the then fledgling Dutch science of Germanic philology. It does not matter that in hindsight a few of his paradigms turned out to be proto-Germanic (e.g., *gemahal,* "spouse") rather than specifically East Germanic. Grotius in particular expressed his belief in the reliability of Jordanes (called by him Jorandes) in his writing on the history of the Goths. The latest study by J. Svennung fully bears him out in his basic assumptions.[78] This is of significance to Old Germanic philology, because Jordanes only summarized the historical findings of his predecessor, Cassiodorus (ca. 485–580) in his *Chronica*. Bishop Isidore of Sevilla's original account of the Visigothic tribe in Spain, to which he himself seems to have belonged, helped in his own mind to bring clarity into a novel feeling of Spanish nationalism *(laus Hispaniae)*.[79] This Scandinavian chronicle is closed by Bishop Paulus Warnfrid's *Deeds of the Langobards,* suggesting to his readers that all of these tribes hailing from ancient Scandinavia attested to the present government's antiquity. Accordingly, ancient and contemporary Sweden was justified in her claim to fame, being as ancient as Rome and older than England and France. Situated north of the Germanic Empire, Old Sweden-Denmark-Norway played a civilizing role comparable to the one depicted in his *Annals and Histories* with respect to Batavians west of the same empire.

The *Historia Gotthorum, Vandalorum & Langobardorum* was immediately reprinted both at Amsterdam and in Paris in 1656, until it found its only translation into Swedish as *Norlandz Chronika* at Visingö in 1670.[80]

Chapter Five
Legal Treatises
Neo-Latin

Ecclesiastic (Church Governance) Law. While Grotius was a young advocate and a state historiographer of Holland, he boasted about his Old Hollanders' religious piety as it was practiced in antiquity. Now, twelve years later, he rubbed more than just "the patina" off[1] this exalted piety by commenting on his contemporaries' controversial piety in the province. When he wrote *Ordinum Pietas* [The States' Dutifulness] he was between two government jobs. He had been elected, but not yet appointed, city governor of Rotterdam, and had not yet resigned his post as attorney general of Holland and West Friesland. Moreover, the States General and Oldenbarnevelt had sent him on a special mission to London, lasting from March to May 1613. During an official encounter with King James I Grotius tried in vain to persuade the monarch that there was cause to draw a parallel between the Counter-Remonstrant faction in the Netherlands and the Puritans of Scotland, whom James disliked. The Puritans were suspect according to James's theological standards, and Grotius wanted the king to cast an equally suspicious glance at the Counter-Remonstrant party across the Channel. James, however, frowned the other way instead, for he was too sharp a theologian to be convinced by this fabrication.

One of the principal Counter-Remonstrant adherents was the Calvinist theology professor Franciscus Gomarus, who taught at Leiden University from 1594 to 1611. In disgust over a rival's appointment, he resigned his chair. This other theologian, chosen on the suggestion of Uitenbogaert, was professor Conrad Vorstius (1569–1624). His appointment was sharply criticized by theologians from the States of Friesland, and even by James I, who suspected Vorstius of heresy, then a serious crime. This particular appointment Grotius tried in vain to whitewash in his *Pietas,* which his mentor, Uitenbogaert, rapidly translated into extremely readable and almost inflammatory Dutch.[2] Out of filial piety Grotius did not admit in either version that one of the three appointing regents was his own father, Dr. jur Jan de Groot. Had he dwelled on this possible conflict of interest, inevitably the conclusion would have been drawn that the attorney general himself had been involved with Vorstius's appointment from the start. Even before Grotius had set foot in England, King James, a "heretical" king by papal standards, had decided that Vorstius, to whom he referred as "this blasphemous monster," was not going to teach theology at Leiden. As defender of the reformed faith His Majesty did not wish to see a heretic teach reformed theology at that illustrious and leading university with its many foreign students, including quite a few from Scotland. During this decade (1610–20) more foreign than Dutch students enrolled at Leiden. Students from Britain ranked third in number.[3] Accordingly, appointments of theological professors at Leiden were scrutinized by fellow theologians. Arminius's successor, Dr. Vorstius, and Gomarus's successor, Dr. Simon Episcopius, a personal friend to Grotius, were liberal with respect to dogma adhered to by the more orthodox reformed church.[4] Franeker University's leading orthodox reformed theologian, Dr. Sibrandus Lubbertus,[5] a native from Friesland, chose to criticize the ultraliberal appointment, and singled out Vorstius's questionable stand on predestination. Lubbertus maintained that, by orthodox standards, Vorstius was not qualified to profess theology at Leiden. He argued further that it was not simply up to the regents of a university alone to pass judgment on a public minister's suitability to profess. The issue of debate became: who was to be the "magistrate" with the power of appointment and removal—the States of Holland in their dutiful conduct, or the Dutch Reformed Church and their bishops in their orthodox wisdom?

Grotius, the regents at Leiden, and the States of Holland in this question were convinced "territorialists." The magistrate in whose territory, and hence jurisdiction, the said appointment to the faculty fell, was felt to have acted as a dutiful public servant of God. Then, if the allegations were proven right, this government magistrate would have to remove from office a controversial theology professor. This was precisely what the Gomarist faction, whose concern Lubbertus voiced, demanded. Fire the heretic and send him away! For they adhered to a "presbyterian" concept of magistracy. The faith of Calvinist clergymen or professors of theology had become an ecclesiastical matter, subject to the presbyters' judgment. It was, in dry words, up to the Dutch Reformed Church, or if the issue could not be resolved, up to a synod to be assembled,[6] to pronounce and then define heretical fallacies.[7] There was in the eyes of Grotius a danger that such a synod might set up a level above the States of Holland; but King James supported the Counter-Remonstrant view in this political entanglement. He was successful in his interference via his ambassador at The Hague, in that the Leiden regents were pressurized to forbid Dr. Vorstius actually to teach theology. He enjoyed a sabbatical, wrote, drew his salary, but could not lecture. While Grotius was still in London, he threw the gauntlet at Dr. Lubbertus, and shortly after his return engaged in a fight of words, "a feud," that was compared to Virgil's fistfight between Dares and Entellus[8] both by his friends and his opponents.[9] The very notion, *pietas,* is the epitheton ornans of father Aeneas.[10] *Pietas,* then, is both a literary and an ecclesiastic term, narrowly speaking, rather than a mere dogmatic notion. Grotius's defense of Holland's dutifulness appeared under two titles which do not quite match. *Pietas* should have been translated by Uitenbogaert into *godsvruchticheyt* in the meaning of "dutifulness," not by *godsdiensticheyt* ("religion") alone. At least in his *States' Parallels* Grotius himself made the distinction between *religio* and *pietas.*[11]

Uitenbogaert was at the time of this strife still court predicant of Prince Maurits and his retainers, and the diatribe published in two languages seemed for a while to represent the majority opinion, all the more so since the States of Holland succeeded in suppressing S. Lubbertus's response to Grotius's attack by an edict in 1614. Thereupon the offended pamphletist from Franeker consulted the Academies of Geneva and Heidelberg, and knit a formidable opposition against Grotius and the Remonstrant party.[12]

Grotius's challenging pamphlet on Holland's piety is written in the tone of a prosecuting attorney. This inflammatory public plea breaks down into five parts:

Legal Treatises

1. (pp. 1–25 of the Dutch version) Polemic: Apology: we, the dutiful Hollanders, have appointed a perfectly sound Calvinistic professor of theology in C. Vorstius. You vindictive attacker succeeded in having his *venia legendi*[13] withdrawn. So, he will be silenced for the time being. But we will not ban his works, nor will we throw him out of the country. There is no law on the books requiring his banishment. Is not your Friesland, Sibrand, full of anabaptists, and do you throw them out of *your* state? *We* have done no wrong! 2. (pp. 25–44) on tolerance: It is the policy of the States of Holland officially to engage in a stance of tolerance on confessional differences, particularly in the dogmatic area of "providence" and "predestination."[14] Grotius, following up on Lubbertus's *Declaration* (1611), directed against Vorstius's orthodoxy, and on his *Commentaries* (1613) dedicated to the archbishop of Canterbury, by his refutation aimed at King James himself. By illustrating the Remonstrant philosophy involved, Grotius in the public mind became associated with their cause, despite the fact that he never officially joined their ranks as a church member. 3. (pp. 44–80) on the "magistrate": Grotius pleads in favor of Holland's right to exert her full ecclesiastic authority, the so-called *jus magistratus*. He goes very far in his "territorial" leanings, certainly as far as Lipsius had gone in respect to possible ecclesiastical enforcement of law at Leiden,[15] and as far as the French Gallicanists and the English apologists of ecclesiastical policy had gone. Lubbertus, on the other hand, was a presbyterian or confessionalist in respect to ecclesiastic discipline.[16] Grotius again tries to push his Counter-Remonstrant adversary into the camp of the Puritans, and vividly paints their negation of a state's right to exert control in all visible church matters. 4. (pp. 80–118) on preventing a schism: Now he tries to document that the Gomarists' theory of "collateral powers," concerning the two regiments within one state, is ill-founded, dangerous, and prone to create a schism within the Reformed Dutch Church. The government magistrate appoints and dismisses, and even excommunicates individual members, and, if need be, calls for a synod. 5. (pp. 118–26) final argument: There are various scales on the hierarchy of ecclesiastical offices. Although his pamphlet was dashed off hurriedly in good faith, Grotius apparently had no foreboding that his opponents would point the sword he himself had forged at his own throat less than five years later, after the Stadholder

had determined to switch sides to the more numerous Counter-Remonstrants, and have the Remonstrant leaders arrested on charges of partially ecclesiastical high treason.

Grotius's state theory of dutifulness proved extremely slippery ground. For his positions held within a member territory of a Confederation contained political inconsistencies. Either one was a territorialist in ecclesiastical as in secular matters, and tried officially to contain rivaling sects, or one was a confessionalist fighting for the principle of mutal tolerance within one state. But not both at the same time! Either one argued publicly for the advantages of a unified Calvinist state-supervised church, was prepared to define a rivaling sect as potentially hostile to the state regimen, or one went along with dismissing a heretical predicant or professor of theology for the sake of public peace, if the peace *was* really threatened.[17] In other words, either one was a public adherent of a unified state church and the consequences, or one wished ultimately to head in the direction of potentially up to seven different Calvinist State churches. It was Grotius who did not grasp the weight of unwritten confederate ecclesiastical law: as a public official one could favor tolerance of intolerance, and thus be triumphantly tolerant by Holland's standards, or one could be intolerant of tolerance, and become public enemy number two, after Johan van Oldenbarnevelt, in the eyes of the people. Grotius committed a political error, the mistake of having the magistrate act for the protection of a minority only, rather than act for the benefit of the majority, too. He failed to create a common assent toward a Hollandic ecclesiastical policy as balanced against Dutch Church order. Holland's officially stated appointment policy of piety (or official good faith) turned into an impiety, at least in the eyes of the orthodox majority, and finally also of the secular ad-hoc court.

Grotius himself said in his *Pietas Ordinum* (Dutch version, 60): "But if one can't do what one wants, one wants to do what one can." This is precisely the direction the more and more vociferous majority was heading for, a decision finally also taken by a special secular-ecclesiastic court, springing from a synod, as "the only medicine to cure all religious sicknesses" (128). The attorney general of Holland in his defense chose to address too many parties at home and abroad. He wanted to vindicate the good faith of his State; he wanted to placate the dissenters and the critics on both sides, and at the same time prevent a schism. He wanted to impress and pull over to his side the archbishop of Canterbury and King James, the highest ranking Reformed prince of Christendom. Was not what Grotius argued for expressed by the most outstanding English theologians all along?[18] Yes, but Holland was not England, the United Provinces not like Britain, the Stadholder not a monarch! In summarizing, we may say that Grotius in vain tried to tamper with regulating very complicated ecclesiastical liberties without having a parliamentary Act of Uniformity on the books. He thus was stirring dangerous waters. Instead of going along with the custom of the church defining who was a heretic, with the magistrate, upon proof, punishing the offender, Grotius wanted to have it the other way around: the States of Holland insisted on defining who was a tolerable dissenter and whom the magistrate did not wish to dismiss. Besides, Holland failed to come out in favor of the synod and thus left it up to the closing ranks of the orthodox to press for a synod on their confederate terms. This would lead to the prosecution and eventually persecution of the whole "offending faction," i.e., the Remonstrant party, of which Grotius had become the nominal head in 1617. It was ironic that by 1618 these practitioners of dutifulness in their behavior looked like radicals to the opposition.

The freshly appointed city governor of Rotterdam, the only Dutch city which had a Remonstrant majority in parliament at that time (1613–17), must have felt that his latest pamphlet needed systematic improvement and refinement in tone. So he wrote another treatise against what we, for want of a better term, call "presbyterian Calvinism" in terms of church government. The treatise was not directed against the orthodox Counter-Remonstrant faction as a political party, but rather treated the matter from the view of church history: *De Imperio summarum Potestatum circa Sacra* [State Authority over Church Matters], written in 1614 but not published until after Grotius's death (Paris, 1647). The historical notion of church law, *circa sacra* (concerning the secular control of sacred things in the church), did not emanate from the political practice of the reformation, but from Reformed theology as taught by Professor Pareus at the University of Heidelberg. The kernel of this notion is found in the formula *potestas regia circa ecclesiastica,* i.e. the regal-governmental power over visible, and thus external, matters within the Reformed Protestant Church.[19] These were, and still are, dogma, sermon, the key to salvation, and the sacraments, to name only the most important ones. These ecclesiastic functions of the church do not aim at abridging the individual Calvinist's freedom of conscience. The two Calvinist factions on either side of the controversy did not deny the spiritual liberty of their adherents before God. Where the split occurred and hatred set in was the dispensation of salvation. For it was dispensed within the framework of civil ecclesiastical law, which at that time was neither all secular nor nonreligious. It was deliberated, both sides thought, enacted and enforced on earth, but very definitely under heaven.[20] It was meant, in other words, to redress the imbalance between our limited knowledge of God and of ourselves. And who possessed such knowledge? The elected, thought the Gomarists; no, all true believers, thought the Arminians. What was the difference?

Grotius had at that time a superficial knowledge of Richard Hooker's (1554–1600) *Of the Laws of Ecclesiastical Polity,* which this Oxford fellow wrote in English, not in Latin.[21] Grotius wanted to iron out the difficulties surrounding ecclesiastical state power on the basis of Holy Scripture and of natural reason as well, and, to top it all, even from the pronouncements of foremost philosophers. In Chapter 1, he works out a theory of Christian consensus,[22] operative since early Christianity. In Chapter 2, he discerns the essence of supreme authority by law of nature now said to have emanated under God. In Chapter 3, he demonstrates the freedom of thought, and the limits ecclesiastical power put over it during the first centuries of Christianity; Chapter 4: the pastoral office of Christ does not overthrow the authority of the highest state government, once it became state religion; 5: the sources for judgments in cases on conflicts, such as scripture, prayer, piety, rectitude, and reason; 6: on preservation of unity in the Church; 7a: the definition, the office of synods, and their possible remedies; b: judgment by and appeals to synods; 8a: ecclesiastical legislation; b: the mitigation of divine laws by the concept of equity; 9: jurisdiction by canonical acts, e.g., concerning the apostolic rod, the use of the keys, etc.; the role of consent in finding ecclesiastical justice; 10: on the election of pastors (= predicants) and the principal steps: mandate, election, ordination, and confirmation, with historical and contemporary illustrative examples; 11: about the offices or institution of bishops, presbyters, lay elders, and pastors;[23] 12: a word of caution on the tether of tolerance, customary in Holland since ancient times.

In our opinion, it is a pity that this treatise on ecclesiastic moderation, pointing out, as it did, Christian roads to salvation with the help of ecclesiastical authority under God, never appeared in our writer's lifetime. It would have carried his political fortune much further than the impassioned plea for Holland's official piety, a broadside by comparison. Now Grotius the savant tries, as Hooker had done before him,[24] to make sure that the Dutch Reformed Church would not deviate from the practice of other reformed churches, particularly not from the relatively peaceful Anglican Church.[25] His *State Authority* represents, in a fashion, a "union program" which during the customary circulation stage among friends, and those whom Grotius mistook for friends, did not please either faction. The pamphlet he published prematurely in 1613 offended, however, only his Calvinist adversaries. The treatise written in 1614, and publishable by 1615, would have done the writer full justice. For the unpublished manual on church law would have proved to the liberals in the country that Grotius was not a radical despite his choice of an inflammatory style in 1613. He had simply meant to defend his beloved Holland from the unfounded charge of ecclesiastic heresy, by a dose of erudition mixed with arrogance toward the experienced theologian Lubbertus, twice his age. The hour of reconciliation had passed. For "piety" had become less than a mere humanistic exercise of interpretation; it had turned into a weapon wielded in the fight of federal religious policy, if need be, against Holland, the mightiest province, as led by Oldenbarnevelt and Grotius. The weapon was going to decide who had the ultimate say in the highest control of the United Provinces: Maurits.

The Atonement of Christ. The States of Holland were attacked because of their implied attitude of so-called *socinianisterye,* the denying of the Trinity among God, Christ, and the Holy Spirit.[26] Professor Vorstius and, by implication, the regents of the culprit university and, above all, her illustrious alumnus, were openly accused of this "crime." We must remember that, as a young man, Grotius had worked out his Christology in his second drama, *Christus Patiens.*[27] In the dramatist's conviction, Jesus had died innocently, just as he was created an innocent, namely as innocently as an emanation from God would be, according to his *Adamus Exul*.[28] There was no court for or against dramatization in literature other than the court of public taste in seventeenth-century Netherlands. But when a spokesman of government policy, the preponderant one in the Confederation at that time, minced fallacious political arguments, the repudiation was not slow in coming.

The National and, at the same time, International Synod of Dordrecht, taking place against the wish of the State of Holland in 1618–19,[29] ruled among other dogmas on one sensitive dogma in a punitive manner.[30] This particular theory, unfortunately for inceptor and public propagandist, was declared religiously unsatisfactory, biblically ill-founded, and even scientifically contradictory.[31] Briefly stated, it tried to define the mediatory office of Jesus Christ on behalf of mankind. The argument runs as follows: Christ in dying innocently for mankind rendered humanity only a "hypothetical satisfaction." His death on the cross does not do vindicative justice for the fall of mankind. Hence only the acceptance of the exemplary amount of suffering *instar omnium* (vicariously in God's image for the benefit of all in the future) will count in our favor on the judgment day.[32] Thus Grotius legally looks at God as if He were a regent rendering clemency[33] to man as a rebellious subject.[34] First Grotius had defended the official piety of his province, now in 1617 he defended no less than her catholicity; that is, Holland's dutiful nondeviation in an essential, and ecclesiastically explosive, dogmatic point. He tried to prove the opposite of what his opponents accused him of, namely, that his sanctification theory was *anti-socinian*.[35] There is perhaps no greater neuralgic point in all of Christian religion than a thoroughly dogmatic presentation of the trinity among Father, Son, and Holy Ghost. At the breakdown point of his personal health—in his portrait of 1617 he really looks very thin and frail—he vainly outlined the salient points by juridical argumentation, which he tried to superimpose on the political heat of the debate. His notion of God as Calvinist regent meting out justice via a relaxation of the law is not scriptural—on which point the three principal secondary writers, Heppe, Schlüter, and Haentjens agree—but hails from secular Roman law. Accordingly, we took the liberty of rubricating this defense of faith under legal treatises with the subheading "ecclesiastical law." His purpose in publishing this treatise was the same as that of his other church law tracts: to pacify the swelling religious-political strife at home. But by here defining satisfaction as "payment not in kind but in different form" in the sense of a remission of the death command, with a time lag of many generations in between, he overstepped the bounds of piety by a long shot. His enemies did not take long to spot the weak point in his satisfaction theory: ecclesiastically speaking, the Grotian differentiation between God as regent and as offended creditor, challenged by His creatures' disobedience and "remitting sins," was untenable. For his theory contains a nucleus of potential terrorization by the regent. If this sovereign of man wants to make sinning abhorrent to mankind, why bother to command His son to suffer on its behalf, if an ordinary angel could have achieved the same result? Instead of defining Remonstrant-reformed theology, as applicable in the legal area and the political arena, he made himself the magnet for attracting retribution from many hostile sides. Soon the court was going to be packed, which would not even allow him to use pen and paper to defend himself properly.

Now it is twenty-five years ago that the extraordinary court of the States General condemned Grotius by a curious sentence which could be termed an ecclesiastic court-martial.[36] In his last major ecclesiastical treatise, *A Vote for Peace in the Church* (1642), Grotius, the aged exile, applied his utmost acumen to illustrate the wisdom of Psalm 133:1 "Behold, how good and pleasant it is when brothers dwell in unity!" The hostile brothers he wished to reconcile spiritually are the Protestant and the Catholic Church. In this significant ecumenical tract he refutes the Calvinist position on total scriptural inspiration, since undoubtedly were a few books in the Hebrew canon (the historical ones of the Old Testament) which did not claim to have been inspired while written, much less dictated by the Holy Spirit. The hair-splitting strife over man's justification in the eyes of God would stop as soon as both churches would truly recognize that Christ *is* our justice and satisfaction. Hence, Grotius felt, it was advisable to drop the tag *sola fide*[37] from the discussion, since it fed the strife needlessly. A genuinely catholic sense of interpretation demanded that, spiritually, human free will was to be tied to the concept of grace, as the Church Fathers of the first three centuries had recognized. What the structure and the church governance should be was best gathered from that ancient tradition of the first 300-odd years of Christianity. The two confessional branches of Christendom should be reunited under one Roman Pope, endowed with reduced ecclesiastic powers as compared to the powers of the contemporary papal see.

Through their spokesman Philipp Melanchthon (1497–1560)[38] the Protestant faction let it be known that the Protestants could live under such a church government. Both sides, so Grotius thought, had to work out a common consensus on the future hierarchical structure of a government under the umbrella of a unified church. He refutes, with the help of reason alone, several articles of the diehard Protestant faction and invokes the chances of peace in the church, the genuine *pax Christi*. No wonder that in Catholic circles the rumor surfaced that Grotius secretly had become an adherent of the Roman Catholic faith. A noted modern historian could show that the Vatican sent an emissary, the Jesuit theologian Joannes de Lugo, to Grotius in Paris.[39] Although their discussion established that the proponent of church unity was considered "not sufficiently catholic" by his Jesuit interrogator, it becomes obvious that the Calvinists considered him less than sufficiently Calvinist ever since *Peace in the Church* circulated. Several writers attacked him mercilessly from then on, and did not stop even after his death in 1645. All these writers could hold against him was his belief in the possibilities of defining a common and ecumenical ground for a universal Christian faith.

His model for ecclesiastic reunion rested on the assumption that in the Erasmian sense there was no unbridgeable contradiction between the Tridentinian Confession on the side of the Catholics and the Augsburg Confession on the side of the Protestants. Although the gulf has since narrowed a little in several countries, neither side ever dared unequivocally take this creative leap of faith. Grotius tried valiantly, but was rejected by the more ancient branch, and condemned by the junior branch, of the Christian religion at different decades of his life.

Ancient Roman Law: *Annotations to Justinian's Civil Law.* The Greek Emperor Justinian's civil law, the celebrated Corpus Juris Civilis[40] was promulgated in three statutes[41] for the territory of the Greco-Roman or Byzantine Empire, which centered around the city of Constantinople, in A.D. 533 and 534. Since the western Roman Empire had been overrun and conquered by Germanic tribes, this

Legal Treatises 95

capital of the eastern Roman Empire had taken over the function of the ancient government in the West. Thus it is ironic that the crescendo finale in the symphony of the Roman history of law should come from Greek orchestration. As a matter of fact, the Byzantine imperial lawyers were afraid that a permanent loss of the Latin civilization would incur, unless the most outstanding legal traditions were to be preserved in a tongue fast falling into disuse at the Bosporus: *Latina non leguntur!*

Justinian, a son of a Serbian peasant, builder of the Hagia Sophia and the last emperor to master Roman law in its entirety, set up three commissions; accordingly, his law code is divided into three major parts: a. *The Institutes.* They are an elementary but systematic treatise on what constituted civil law at that time. It is a manual promulgated by imperial decree having the force of law, and regulates four areas: (1) the law of persons; (2) the law of things of ownership and possession; (3) the law of contracts and torts; (4) the law of legal remedies and procedure.[42] b. The second and most voluminous part of this Byzantine law code is referred to as *Digests.*[43] This text contains fifty books of unequal length, arranged by legal area. The texts are literally excerpts from the decisions of approximately forty western Roman lawyers whom Emperor Justinian's commission considered outstanding and whose opinions consequently were thought of as authoritative in the practice of law. Hence the *Digests* constitute Roman common law to which the promulgation in A.D. 533 gave legal standing. By implication, the omitted opinions were officially deprecated, and soon doomed to oblivion, until they were resurrected by fourteenth-century Bolognese law professors again. c. The third part of this law corpus, called the (second) *Codex,* selects decisions and edicts, formerly codified by various western Roman emperors until 534, up to and including the one from the East, in excerpt form and is arranged in twelve books. This *Codex* falls into legal titles and paragraphs. This tripartite legal monument, written in a language foreign to the Greeks, survived in this Hellenized form the old Roman Empire, and ultimately became the model for the fourteenth-century canonical law code and for secular *Reichsrecht* (German imperial law) in sixteenth-century Germany. Grotius was familiar with the whole gamut of Roman private law.[44]

His *Annotations to Justinian's law* (Paris, 1642) is a fruit of his lifelong labors with Roman law, which he started to paraphrase in hexameters as early as 1599.[45] These annotations were kept by Grotius in prose form; only the Latin title, *Florum Sparsio* (literally, "the strewing of ornamental flowers"), is poetic. The title, however, is a *captatio benevolentiae* on the part of Grotius. This collection excerpts comments from ancient philosophers, orators, poets, historians, grammarians, further legal commentators, and even occasionally from Holy Scripture. It is the point of that book to elucidate the meaning of a particular legal phrase or of a whole paragraph.[46] Thus we are entitled to call these annotations a chain commentary for the settling of legal-historical arguments. These collections of parallel passages are not meant to be used directly in any court, but rather are of interest to the scholar of Roman jurisprudence. In respect to the *Institutions* Grotius selectively comments on two-thirds of the mass of the titles contained in the four books. In his remarks on the *Digests,* he actually comments on selections from the entire fifty books; and in his discussion of the *Codex* he omits none of the twelve books from his selective list.

In order to illustrate his annotative method we choose two key legal terms, namely "justice" and "jurisprudence" as used in the Corpus Juris. Grotius wanted to check whether the main body of this codification used them consistently, and found that it did. At the very beginning of the *Institutes* (I, 1,1) "justice" is defined as "constant and perpetual desire to render everyone his due." This definition reappears in *Digests* (I, 1,10.2). "Jurisprudence," on the other hand, is defined as "the knowledge of divine and human matters,"[47] and is identical with what we understand by "science of law." Do other leading Greek and Latin writers agree with those definitions? In his subsequent comments on the *Digests* (e.g., 57 ff.) he lists other sayings on the two terms, and various disagreements. He then checks the derivation of "the just" (conformable to the law) which interests him.[48] Reading a few of these comments it becomes evident that Grotius in his study is really interested in the literal meaning of the law and that his methodic aim is to restore the law at least abstractly to its purest possible version. He truly works as a legal-historical *glossator*. The modern editors, according to Dumbauld,[49] accepted several dozens of his emendations, mostly in the *Digests*.[50] Grotius does not intend to decide which of the various definitions are the most apt ones; rather, he is mindful of the philologically correct ones. Then he regularly compares convincing

Legal Treatises

readings to the fundamental juridical problems involved in reference to each other. In essence, some of these approaches to defining legal principles of Roman law on a comparative basis are still viable today.[51]

International Art of War Studies. Hollander by birth, Grotius had a special reverence for the sea. As a student at Leiden he liked to ride horseback on the shore of the North Sea near the beach of Katwijk. His oldest writing is an "oration in praise of navigation" from 1591. Only twice, however, did he undertake a sea voyage, the first to England in the spring of 1613, which cost him King James's good will and ultimately his career; the second one, on the return leg from Stockholm to Lübeck, in the summer, of 1645, claimed his life in the aftermath of a shipwreck. As a writer he devoted Chapter 21 of his *States' Parallels* to maritime matters and seafaring. A little later, according to W. van Eysinga,[52] he started to formulate a lengthy commentary on the just seizure of spoils, particularly in the far seas.[53]

The Freedom of the High Seas. This work was commissioned by the United Dutch East Indies Company (= VOC) because of the capture of the Portuguese caravel *Sta. Catharina* in the Moluccas 25 February 1603. Several such captures had occurred before on both sides, but this one by the Dutch admiral Heemskerck had been taken on behalf of the VOC and an Amsterdam-based branch of VOC shipowners, constituted something special. The 1,500-ton caravel contained valuables that sold to the tune of 3.4 million guilders. She was brought safely to Holland, and the Council of the Admiralty declared her "good prize" on 9 September 1604. The shareholders on this occasion could expect a twenty percent dividend. In our opinion, Grotius started his commentary on the legal aspects of taking prize at sea after he ceased to be historiographer of Holland and West Friesland in 1604, but before he was promoted to attorney general in 1607, in other words, after the seizure, between 1604–6.

The greater part of the twelfth chapter of this commentary, including slight textual revisions, appeared anonymously very shortly after the successful negotiation of the Spanish-Dutch Twelve-Year Truce, late in April 1609.[54] Grotius joined the ranks of legal writers anonymously as public commentator[55] in an area quite vital to the young Dutch Republic. His incognito was publicly lifted first on the title page of the second Dutch translation of his *Mare Liberum* entitled *Vrye Zeevaert*

(1614). Grotius's caution was well advised, for the book was put on the Catholic Index of Forbidden Books nine months after its appearance, on 30 January 1610.[56]

In order to understand this monograph on freedom of navigation and free trade, one has to comprehend two background problems. One, the partition line agreed upon in 1493–94 by Portugal, Spain, and the Papal See,[57] was no longer enforceable. The conquest of Portugal by Spain in 1580 led to a personal union between the two countries, and thus made this line obsolete. Spanish-Portuguese attempts to monopolize all Atlantic and Indian Ocean navigation were fought by the French, the British, and the Dutch by means of brute force or "piracy." This matter of legally unimpeded navigation did not become internationally settled once and for all until the Treaty of Münster and Osnabrück, Westphalia, in 1648. Portugal and the Netherlands were only indirectly at war during the time of seizure; they were antagonists, insofar as Portugal had been conquered by the Spanish. Thus on the high seas Portuguese vessels were considered hostile. Accordingly, the Dutch court decided that this seizure was "legal" and that this prize was "good." When some of the shareholders, who belonged to the Mennonite sect, felt offended and gave their share to the poor, the problem seized the public imagination whether the spoiling was ethically justifiable. Second, according to the law,[58] a booty taken from an enemy in a war through a naval operation became the property of the state. The VOC, however, was a state within a state, and, navally speaking, the more powerful agency of the two.

Grotius in his *Freedom of the High Seas* chains together two lines of argument: since navigation, according to Grotius, is unimpedable by law of nature, maritime commerce is open to participation by all sea-voyaging nations—a viewpoint France had argued for ever since the sixteenth century. In other words, in this circular argument, the justification of uncontrolled commerce, carried out on the high seas in good faith, was necessarily dependent on the sea's openness to all seafaring.[59]

In his fifth chapter Grotius contrasts the openness of the high seas with the idea of "dominance" or control by a colonial power such as Spain or the fledgling seapower Britain.[60] Grotius rejects their aspirations, whether these are based on papal bulls or on brute force, as

Legal Treatises

contrary to "the divine and immutable law of nature." In Chapter 8 he argues that since no one nation *has* dominance over the sea at large, it follows that the sea is "owned by mankind." The practicality of such a lofty generalization was put to the test only too soon. After negotiations in London between the VOC and the English East India Company (EEIC) on fishery disputes failed, despite Grotius's participation as legal expert, a second British-Dutch conference took place at The Hague, February to May 1615. One of the seven Dutch negotiators was again Grotius. Embarrassingly, the British side argued in favor of unimpeded maritime trade on the basis of the law of nations. Triumphantly, the British negotiators could point at their opponent's *Freedom of the High Seas,* according to which this contested freedom of navigation and maritime commerce could be abrogated only by multilateral, internationally valid agreements.[61] This second conference failed, too, because the Dutch side insisted on the validity of their monopolizing agreements concluded with the natives, excluding British trade, e.g., from the Moluccas. That such treaties were really concluded as alliances reducing the full sovereignty of Asian rulers was denied by the Dutch delegation, and again denied by our delegate ten years later in his *De Jure Belli ac Pacis*.[62]

The *Freedom of the High Seas* developed principles of international law, which neither the VOC nor the EEIC wanted to adhere to at that time. While Grotius was a Dutch government official, the practical freedom of the sea was not interpreted as governed by the law of nature, but rather by the law of nations, or, to put it more pointedly, by might and expediency.[63] At both fishery rights conferences Grotius argued practically in favor of partial dominion, or partial restriction of trade, anticipating the point of view of his future antagonist, John Selden, MP, who was to argue on the basis of *mare clausum* or naval dominance.[64] Although a Dutchman, Grotius argued as a partial Seldenist rather than as abstract Grotian. Concerning the trade in the East Indies Grotius's *Mare liberum* of 1609 could not possibly serve Dutch expansionist colonial policy goals,[65] whereas it may have been of advantage to the mercantile policy of the VOC during the first phase of their operation between 1602–9.

As a tendentious tour de force the *Mare liberum* is a masterpiece of grafting pseudolegal arguments onto practical necessities. He dedicates his tract to "the rulers and the free peoples of Christendom." One wonders where such free people lived outside Utopia. *Freedom of the High Seas* is anti-Machiavellian in tone and appeals to Christian conscience and Christian trade on the seven seas. Why is that freedom a law of nature? Because "God himself pronounces thus in nature."[66] He quotes Virgil[67] and uses the famous phrase *debellare superbos* ("to subdue rebellious uprisers") and at least ten other weighty poetic sources, as well as dozens of writers from many genres and all ages, to prove his point. But all these crafty quotations serve only to back up the second main point of the whole tract: the Dutch vessels have the unimpedable right to trade freely with the East Indians during peace, during a truce, and also during a war. The last poetic quotation used, from Propertius, invokes no less than Emperor Augustus's famous oracle before the battle of Actium (in which he defeated Queen Cleopatra's fleet), in order to pretend that the sea god Poseidon could be mobilized on the side of the honorable seafaring Dutch nation,[68] and make the Netherlands win. Grotius sounds the trumpet of war, if war be unavoidable, at the end of his pamphlet. Therefore, we have to be convinced that *Mare liberum* was deliberately held back from publication during the Truce Conference at The Hague in the spring of 1609, until it was concluded, so as not to embarrass the peace party headed by Oldenbarnevelt.

Out of fairness to Grotius anyone discussing his law of prize and booty has to bear in mind that the twenty-three-year-old lawyer and writer treated it as a private exposé for the VOC, and not as a fully matured, publishable book. As a matter of fact, it must be said at the outset that he drew extensively on the first chapters of this commentary and reworked them into the framework of *De Jure Belli ac Pacis,* as we shall see during our subsequent discussion in this chapter. We may, therefore, only judge it on methodological grounds,[69] and not on stylistic merits, despite the fact that, by general agreement, they are nothing short of admirable.

The fifteen chapters comprising this commentary are arranged under four principal headings: 1. preliminaries; 2. dogmatics: a table of nine rules for the sources of law and their corresponding thirteen norms governing the justifiability of particular wars in the perspective of Christian ethics, the taking of booty during such wars; the sufficient cause for wars, private as well as public;[70] the causes and circumstances

Legal Treatises

of justly waged wars;[71] the purpose and aims of such wars; the rightful recipients of prize and booty; 3. historic Spanish-Dutch-Portuguese entanglements leading to an actual state of war; 4. application of the foregoing to the law of prize; on the freedom of the High Seas; private war and just booty;[72] on the acquisition of just booty by "the company" (= VOC); on the immutable law of nature making such a prize "honorable";[73] and finally on the "expediency" of keeping such an honorable prize.[74]

Since the basic legal assumptions here formulated are retained in the *Law of War and Peace,* we shall defer their discussion until we reach our next point, and only focus here on the dogmatics presented in tabular form in Grotius's Chapter 2, which is dropped as superfluous scholastic formalism from the more mature work. Stripped of their frills, the tabular dogmatics contain the basic elements of Grotius's earliest legal philosophy.[75] A synopsis of these rules reveals that law, whether oral or written, emanates from God,[76] and is to be accepted by common consent expressed by mankind, before it becomes binding on each individual and enforceable by the magistrate. Grotius derives the force of law from a potential trinity formed among God, mankind, and individual. He differentiates between public law, governed by rules of the commonwealth, and private law, governed by the rules of conduct of the individual. The basic dichotomization branches out somewhat as follows:

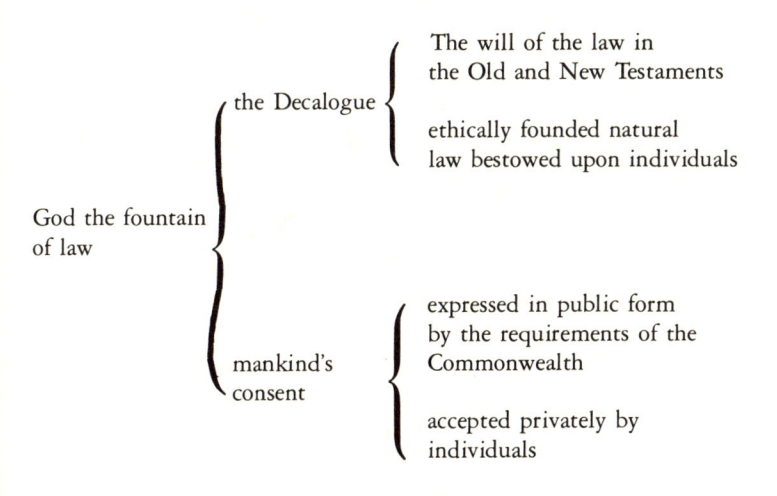

God the fountain of law
- the Decalogue
  - The will of the law in the Old and New Testaments
  - ethically founded natural law bestowed upon individuals
- mankind's consent
  - expressed in public form by the requirements of the Commonwealth
  - accepted privately by individuals

These rules of law are held together by the term "to will" or in Latin *se . . . velle,* implying freedom of choice implanted by God into the human mind. These rules of law are balanced and checked[77] by norms (in Latin, *leges* I–XIII) which could be labeled a rudimentary list of a bill of rights as well as obligations; these are hierarchically emanating from the will of God, too: "by virtue of origin, divine law prevails over human law, and human law over civil law."[78]

In Chapter 3, he ponders the fundamental question, can war ever be just?[79] An affirmative answer by the evidence of God's will is, according to Grotius, found in Nature and expressed in Holy Scripture. It follows that war is permitted after Christ and for Christians. It follows furthermore (Chapter 4) that by the same token the acquisition of prize by right of war is justified also, as long as the war is just. The source of permission is again the law of Nature and the law of Nations. The aim is to collect a just reimbursement for the costs for war. Today we would call such a reimbursement "reparation."

The rest of the book is written from the point of view of a partisan advocate, not free from prejudice, ushering the precious spoil safely into the hands of those thankful shareholders who sponsored this "private" war in the first place. The rest centers around the themes of just grievances and justified redemption. The prize obtained in just private war (see Chapter 13) is finally turned into one justly acquired in the course of a public war.[80] Toward the end of the last chapter, the plea shifts into a startling invocation that in this patriotic enterprise God is on the Dutch side. The ultimate basis for a just prize is really nothing other than the welfare of Holland. No peril without profit, no expenditures without recompensation! "It has pleased Him to select the Dutch in preference to all others . . . so that no fault on their part may render the true religion odious to unconsecrated nations . . . ."[81]

In essence, Grotius argues that taking and keeping prize on the high sea is not simply the antithesis of civilized behavior; and that the process of taking prize could best be adjudged by commercial chambers of the VOC. It has been claimed that the law of prize and booty is the preliminary edition of the *Law of War and Peace.*[82]

The Law of War and Peace. Although Grotius made intensive use of the unpublished manuscript on prize and booty while writing his *Law of War and Peace*, the intellectual thrust and the juridical argumentation of the two treatises are quite unlike each other. Not only does their inception lie twenty years apart; the "Prize" has to justify an act of taking somebody else's property, and therefore it is entirely pragmatic. Its reasoning is directed toward solving self-raised legal questions by legal replies. The argumentation of the "Law of War," on the other hand, tries to enunciate general legal propositions by orderly deductions. Methodically, the "Prize," with its scholastic syllogisms, still belongs to the era of the change from the sixteenth to the seventeenth century; the "War," however, takes geometry and arithmetic for its model, so that the deductionary system presented may be of help in a situation of learning and applying creative law.[83] Here the addressee is ultimately mankind aggrieved by the ravages of war. Grotius talks of the kinds of deductions he has in mind in the Prolegomena (P), the forewords: DJBP P 58: "With all *truthfulness* I aver that, just as *mathematicians treat their figures as abstracted* from bodies, so in treating law I have withdrawn my mind *from* every particular *fact.*" And DJBP P 59: "I have therefore *followed,* so far as I could, *a mode of speaking* at the same time *concise* and suitable for exposition, in order that those who deal with public affairs may have, as it were, *in a single view* both the kinds of *controversies . . . and the principles* by which they may be *decided.*"[84] The two commentaries on booty and war measures share the point of departure; however, they approach their respective solutions quite differently. The "Prize" asks as principal question: can any war be just? The *War and Peace* asks instead: what does the law say about war? The former approach decides a case (ultimately awarding the *Sta. Catharina* to the VOC shareholders again) and solves a particular maritime legal problem exemplarily. The latter in a philosophical manner combines legal sources by working out solutions along the lines of a novel anthropology of law.[85] W. Fikentscher outlined those elements of good versus bad faith that reappear in DJBP,[86] so that there is no need to list them again, and just add a few more connections. From our angle we want instead to expand on the comparison. *The Law of War* (= DJBP), being twice as long as "Prize," quotes and mentions exactly twice as many authors from various fields, but requotes fully half of the 169 names once again.[87]

The understanding of *The Law of War* will be seriously hampered if one thinks for a moment, like modern man does, that peace be the antithesis of war! Grotius, on the contrary, thought that war really was the permissible way to drive judicially toward peace. Thus the law of peace for him is neither a separate category from the law of war, nor is the law of peace the antithesis of the law of war.[88] War, for Grotius, is primarily of legal interest, insofar as it may further civilization, and insofar as it regrettably destroys part of mankind. Grotius's predecessors demythologized the concept of "state" and of "law" by placing the law where it belongs, namely as a force of nature to be checked by the state. He developed the basic precepts for fighting a war started over injuries unjustly received from the enemy;[89] then he examines whether the orbit of the law may reach, sort out, and "tame" war. In fact he tries no less than to subject the totality of supranational[90] relations, and hence war, as its principal expression, *to* the rule of law. He must have been confident that rules dictated by right reasoning could be found and formulated clearly, for he says so in DJBP I, 1, 10,1.

It is generally assumed that the title of Grotius's work was derived from a passage in Cicero's Oration for Balbus, Chapter 6: *universum denique belli jus ac pacis* ("the concise universal law of war and peace"), but it seems equally probable to us that he thought of the thirteenth-century Spanish philosopher Ramon Llull's famous proverb as well: "Justice procures peace and injuries war."[91] In any case, Grotius proceeds from a bridgehead won by reason and bases his deductions on an enormous storehouse of ancient classical knowledge and historical underpinnings. He does this creative work by following the philosophical tenets of the School of the Stoa, which saw in reason a refined form of a sociability. Grotius rephrased the Stoic concept οικειοσις[92] as *appetitus societatis* ("social appetite"). This drive toward organizing a peaceful human society he also poetically circumscribed as "shadow and trace of reason."[93] Grotius wanted to extrapolate no less than the external truth analogous to the mathematical axioms.[94]

In order to retrace and find access to the artistic presentation underlying DJBP, we have to relate a number of *realia* first. The most obvious one is that the subdivisions of the text and the prolegomena in paragraphs, supervised by his son Pieter for the 1667 edition of DJBP (TMD 579), are inauthentic, and may, in our view, mathematically be less than correct.[95] They are ornaments added by a lawyer for lawyers, and are of course very helpful, but not artistically Grotian. Second, our author, just as Goethe, liked to dictate his books while walking, or at least up on his feet. In Baligny-sur-Thérain he dictated to Th. Graswinckel, his brother's nephew,[96] but he dictated from prodigious memory, for he could perform his thoughts while walking outside. In the countryside during the summer of 1623 he could, for the first time undisturbed, walk off the claustrophobia contracted at Loevestein: "I alternately study and walk, and even study while walking."[97] Considering that this was precisely the way he composed poetry in his younger years,[98] we are challenged to uncover DJBP's artistic components as vestiges of this exhilarating creative process, all the more so since, "as a mental type, Grotius, notwithstanding the incredible acuity of his mind, belonged to the unshakable naive ones. . . ."[99] In a literary study such as this one it does not suffice to marvel at and repeat with van Eysinga that "the Grotian conception, the beauty of its language and the structure of this work of art moves in both classical and Christian spheres and leaves an impression as Dante's Divina Commedia."[100] Such a structure, if existent, has to be demonstrated.

We found by comparing DJBP's structure with that of DJPr, in 1604, and all of the three dramas from 1601, 1608, and also of 1634, that it is conceived as and based upon the principal scheme of FIVE. "The letter five is the sign of the law; and of the Pentateuch, of the . . . Old Testament," and of "the fivefold partition of the passion of Christ." "Fifty," the total number of all the chapters of Books II and III of DJBP together, "serves like the *annus jubilaeus* in Leviticus 25:10," ". . . to institute a phase of peace."[101] But most strikingly, the Roman legal model for Grotius's DJBP was Justinian's *Digests,* which is organized in fifty books. Furthermore, "five as a circular number" is also ". . . the type of nature," "the first perfect number."[102] "Five" constitutes a "category of abstraction" operative ". . . for notions . . . from different spheres of culture."[103] "Five" stands ". . . for a conduct of life oriented toward charity of one's fellow man."[104] Accordingly, Grotius keeps the five-chapter arrangement of *De Jure Praedae Commentarius,* which is based on a multiple of three, amounting to fifteen chapters,[105] in DJBP: Book I contains five chapters. Book II contains five main blocks, enlarged by the factor of five. Book III contains three main points enlarged by the factor of six (plus two interludes or digressions). Grotius invokes the truthfulness of beautiful order in Prolegomenon

58. The Pythagorean[106] in Grotius, as it were, owes his method, by which the particular arrangement proceeds from the universal one, to a growth from FIVE to SIX: Dante, Paradiso, XV, 55–57: "You deem that to me your thought must flow/from primal thought, as out of unity,/well studied, five and six are seen to grow."

The Prolegomena must have been dictated after the completion of the work on the main body; for these forewords go over the outline of the whole body in a double cursus, first, macrocosmically, and second, microcosmically, in analogy to the Stoic teaching of the first and the second nature of man.

Remarks by van Eysinga[107] and Huizinga[108] made the point that DJBP was an attempt to give jurisprudence the form of an art. It should be regarded as *kunstwerk* with all its "polyphonic qualities" and be judged "by its severe form and august ideal." In other words, the great Huizinga pleads that Huigh de Groot here tried to cast the beauty of truth into an aesthetic form. All we are trying to do is to recapture some of this deep structure, as imperfectly as it must read on paper.

In order to appreciate the structure of the five main units of DJBP we can see the musical quality of it, too:

1. warfare in view of the law (basically overlapping with Book I)
2. a catalogue of rights, potentially leading to justified warfare and enforcement of peace (until Chapter 20 of Book II)
3. from unjust to doubtful reasons for warfare (Chapters 22 ff. of Book II)
4. compelling rules versus rights for fighting legitimate war
5. measures short of war; moderation and neutrality and minimal good faith between enemies.

The main theme (1) is broken up and played through by a fugue, expressed in counterthemes (2) and (4), the compelling rights, interrupted as well as rounded off by the contrapuntal subsidiary theme (3), and the restrictions leading to mitigations aiming at charity (5).

Legal commentators and the future editor of the as yet not existing critical edition[109] will want to take heed of this artistic, structurally verifiable concept expressed by Grotius in the internal rhythm and spacing of his text in 1625. It is made of the spirit connecting war and human progress. The famous Spanish artist Diego Velasquez caught it in his oil painting *The Honorable Surrender of Breda*. The underlying act of grace extended by the otherwise merciless General Spinola was granted to the beleaguered Breda in 1625, the year when DJBP appeared. Grotius's creative conception of what the law of regulating ferocious European and colonial warfare could achieve kindled an intellectual fire of enthusiasm throughout educated circles in Europe. King Gustavus Adolphus, Richelieu, Cardinal Bellarmine, and countless law professors admired DJBP. A Hugo Grotius chair of law was established in Heidelberg and, with a recommendation of Hugo's son Pieter, offered to Dr. Samuel Pufendorf, who accepted it at age twenty-nine in 1661. A new branch of legal inquiry had been born. Grotius liberated the law of nations *(Völkerrecht)* from obscurity and disdain. Eternally valid sentences, as if they had the character of an immediately plausible mathematical theorem, stand in the seminal book, as pleaders of the better, the ethical spirit of the seventeenth century:

For justice brings peace of conscience, while injustice causes torments and anguish . . . (Prol. 20); Natural law is the dictate of right reasoning . . . (I, 1, 10); Let the laws be silent then in the midst of arms, but only the laws of the state, . . . not those other laws, which are of perpetual validity and suited to all times (Prol. 26); One may never forget that the commands of charity reach further than those of the law. (III, 13,4,1)

These and countless other theorems found in the main body give DJBP the character of a concordance on teaching toleration, or at least limited warfare amidst total belligerency. Although Grotius is not militarily speaking a pacifist at all, it is ironically that misconception which founded the world-wide reputation of his book, and made it a classic of international law, supposedly valid for the citizenry of the world,[110] experiencing mankind's hope against oppressive ideologies which preceded the appearance of this treatise on arbitrating war into an instrument of peace. It can also bring intellectual vigor to any reader weighed down by the fatigue of the rigors of the Hobbeses, and other neo-Machiavellian thinkers and their modern creatures. His axioms, it seems to us, are articulating the sighs of the collective mind at odds with incarcerating positivistic law. The moral examples presented are siphoned from Roman law, Christian church fathers, the Bible, ancient historians, philosophers, and last but not least, poets. In keeping with the structure, dominated by the figure "five," the methodology applied in DJBP is an open one par excellence. *The Law of War and Peace* was written by a political exile who was at home in the literary republic as well as in the kingdom of divinity. He vindicated the concept of war after the ravages of the Eighty Years' War. By working out the structure of the law of war, he helped increase mankind's chances for peace.

Dutch

Holland's Institutes: **An Introduction to Dutch Jurisprudence.** Of all of Grotius's writing in jail (1619–21) this treatise is the most tightly organized piece. One has to imagine the circumstances: the ex-attorney general who had never bothered formally to study law at a university,[111] who had fallen from the highest legal office the land could bestow, and received a lifelong prison sentence, now took intellectual revenge in a devastating way: lacking the aid of his cherished legal library, which had been confiscated,[112] he sat down nevertheless and wrote the first modern Roman-Hollandic law treatise, by amalgamating Justinian's *Institutes* with Old Dutch customs, charters, and bylaws partially from memory; and he did it in Dutch enriched by many terms of his own coinage. The outcome is a tract one could dub "Proof of civil Dutch law," parallel to his "Proof of Christian Religion," which we discussed in the second chapter. He single-handedly proved that Holland's Institutes, as systematized by him, set precedent and standard for a general introduction to Dutch jurisprudence in all the other provinces, too. In our title we want to make the point that his *Institutes* try to preempt Dutch jurisprudence of his time and for the future. He worked at the archetype manuscript which he must have dictated to Willem Corneliszoon v.d. Velde, as he had *Geloof's Voorberecht,* the original manuscript of *Bewijs van den waeren Godsdienst.*[113] After a copy by his scribe, who was the only one with him at Loevestein who could both spell accurately and write a good hand, had been completed, the original was burned so that it would not fall into the hands of his censors. After a careful checking process in liberty outside, Willem de Groot, a young lawyer himself, published the *Inleidinghe tot de Hollandsche Rechts-geleertheyd* (TMD 757) at The Hague in the spring

Legal Treatises

of 1631. During that same year three more editions sprang up in several Dutch cities without authorization from the Grotius brothers. Well nigh every lawyer of rank wished to study this eminent Dutch-written work on the civil law of Holland.

The system of presentation is so tightly Ramistic[114] that every paragraph evolves from principal notions to branching into the most specialized regulations. He always first defines the principal arguments and leads the user to a juridical dissection of the main and the subsidiary problems in the area of civil law.[115] As a key to comprehension he attaches to the main body *five* well-spaced synoptic tables which are governed, and thus prefaced, by the following five uppermost terms:

1. the art of jurisprudence   governing BOOK I, 1–10
2. the legal condition of man   governing BOOK I, 11–15
3. the legal condition of things   governing BOOK II, 1–13
4. possessions and ownership[116]   governing BOOK II, 14–48
5. obligations and claims   governing BOOK III, entire

These five principal legal institutes govern the civil law in lieu of a separate prolegomenon.[117] Book I is structured on a multiple of three in fifteen chapters. Books II and III together have exactly one hundred chapters, "the number of perfection."[118] Grotius originally planned to write a Book IV on the law of civil procedural remedies. But instead he decided to refer his users to Paul Merula's standard work on procedure which had just appeared.[119] This "strict symmetry" runs through Grotius's *Inleidinghe* as a "red thread"; the "Hollandic parts" are blended in harmoniously.[120] His symmetrical harmonization can best be apprehended from the modern retranslation of the text into Latin.[121] Grotius, in any case, is fully justified when he claims in the prefaced letter version to his sons that he took particular care in *arranging* this Roman-Hollandic civil law system ". . . certainly as well ordered as in Justinian's Institutes." He also wanted to prove, and completely succeeded in proving, that seventeenth-century Dutch was well suited for legal science. He stresses ". . . that some words were formed by me through conglomeration and by going back to good old Dutch words fallen in oblivion."

Dr. Magda Esch-Pelgroms in a regrettably almost unknown Liège thesis demonstrates that of the 508 special legal terms used by Grotius in *Inleidinghe,* 221 are still viable. Only nobody realizes that of these, sixty-eight are original creations by our defender of the *Nederduitse taal.*[122] This is an enormously rich legacy left to his sons, to his ungrateful country, and ultimately to Roman-Dutch, Netherlandic, and Belgian law.[123] It distills centuries of legal experience into living language. As a law, according to Grotius's legal mind, can have three effects—(1) to create obligation, (2) to prescribe punishment for violation, and (3) to nullify acts conflicting with the law[124]—a well-executed law book, according to Grotius's artistic mind, should have created gratitude on the part of the recipients, help to revoke undeserved punishment, and nullify acts of persecution directed against the author by leading Dutch lawyers of his time. He privately expressed the hope that his Hollanders would "send him a ship to bring him home."[125] Fourteen years later the City Government of Amsterdam chartered a ship indeed, but for a transit passage to Sweden, where he had to take leave from his diplomatic service as peacemaker. It was to be a sea voyage of no return. The Dutch Demosthenes shipwrecked and died abroad.

Chapter Six
Critical Evaluation
The Man in His Time

His Correspondence. Of Grotius's main works, all except the third drama, *Joseph in Egypt*, the Dutch version of "Proof of Christian Religion" *(Bewijs)*, the *Inleidinghe*, and two Greek textbook editions were put on the Index of Forbidden or Expurgated Books by the Spanish Inquisition, or were at least put up for partial correction. In the eyes of the Catholic church officials, his works, albeit plainly arguing for peacefulness, were not catholic enough, and hence remained too controversial. But they were debated and analyzed by the educated people of Europe, particularly in the Netherlands, Germany, England, and France. Cardinal Richelieu is reported to have recognized only three true scholars in his lifetime. Two were Frenchmen and the third one was Grotius, then working in Paris. For the writer of controversially famous books it was natural that he should belong to the literary republic of scholars who regularly corresponded world-wide. This age of frequent letter writing exchanged points of view on every question of literary taste and also on intelligence data, and usually on a mixture of both, since both issues were of vital consequence.

The most prolific letter writer of the period ending in the first decade of the seventeenth century was professor Justus Lipsius from Brussels, whom we came across in Chapter 2. According to G. Oestreich[1] he had some 700 correspondents, and held the reputation that this number made him the outstanding letter writer of Europe in his time. Concerning his disciple Grotius, 5,000 letters have been printed so far, encompassing the period from 1597–1640, and 2,400 more letters covering the years 1641–45 are being readied for publication by the Grotius Institute at The Hague. Another 200 letters dating from his youth had been omitted and will be incorporated in the reprinting of vols. 1 and 2 of the *Briefwisseling*. Before the end of the 1980s, some 7,650 letters to and from Grotius will be available.[2] The number of correspondents until 1640 who are known by name has, according to our statistic from the files of the Grotius Institute, reached 306. A table with tentative data looks like this:

HUGO GROTIUS CORRESPONDENCE

Name	Years	No.	From HG	To HG	Total
Willem de Groot (brother)	1614–45	1.	822	178	±1000
Nicolaas van Reigersbergh (brother-in-law)	1608–39	2.	474	243	717
Axel Oxenstierna (Swedish chancellor)	1633–42	3.	259	41	300
Ludwig Camerarius (pfälz. envoy, The Hague)	1635–45	4.	175	0	175
Gerard J. Vossius (friend and professor)	1613–45	5.	158	65	223
B. Aubéry du Maurier (French ambass. Hague)	1614–36	6.	91	30	121
Dan. Heinsius (boyhood friend)	1602–14	7.	88	8	96
Joh. A. Salvius (Swed. agent Hamburg)	1635–45	8.	78	54	132
P. Schmalz (Sec. to Oxenstierna)	1635–38	9.	60	1	61
Christina, Queen of Sweden	1635–44	10.	39	17	56
St. Bielke (Swed. ambass. Germany)	1636–38	11.	39	8	47
Jan de Groot (father)	1608–40	12.	38	19	57
C. Marini (agent for Sweden)	1634–40	13.	36	200	236
G. M. Lingelsheim (pfälz. professor)	1605–31	14.	35	14	49

Critical Evaluation

I. Köhne v. Jasky (Dantzig professor)	1636–42	15.	32	32	64
I. Casaubonus (Swiss philologist)	1602–14	16.	23	30	53

We carried these letter statistics up to correspondent number 34 by frequency of letters *by* Grotius, and found that 55 percent of the total correspondence passed between him and 10 percent of the total number of his correspondents. To this selective group—in which his wife occupies only place twenty—Grotius wrote twice as many letters as he received. Even his letters addressed to his relatives are always issue-oriented. More than one-seventh are filled by his official "Swedish" correspondence, and contain diplomatic as well as intelligence data. The correspondence increases in volume from the time of his Swedish appointment (1634).[3] Although he was a master stylist of formal as well as telegram-style letter writing, it is evident, after reading a representative sample of his predominantly Latin letters, that the total correspondence which was preserved is distinctly secondary in importance to his works, and does not tell decisively more than one already knows from his work habits and literary preferences. One trait, however, needs stressing: he was a slave driver when it came to completing a pending publication. He rarely read final proof himself, even while he was not yet an exile or refugee. His three principal proofreaders were Daniel Heinsius until 1612–13, Willem de Groot and G. J. Vossius, both from 1614–15 until 1645. Late in the 1640s, Vossius's son Isaac took over until after Grotius's death. Pieter de Groot, a lawyer and high government official by then, supervised the proofreading of Grotius's posthumously edited works.

Psychologically, Grotius was on more intimate terms with two older scholarly friends, Lingelsheim (Heidelberg/Strassburg) and Casaubonus (Royal Librarian of James I) being the most important ones, than with his family members, except for his younger brother Willem, whose patience has to be admired. Although two modern editors took the trouble to edit and publish Marie van Reigersbergh's correspondence,[4] it has become obvious that only her letters to him breathe spontaneous feelings of love. This usual lack of expressing warm feelings for his wife openly in letters is in all likelihood related to young Hugo's aloofness toward his mother.[5] Summarizing our reading of a representative sample from both his Latin and his Dutch correspondence, we are of the opinion that Grotius's correspondence is businesslike, formal, courteous, factual, gathering and giving military information, diplomatic[6] and scholarly in tone, or apologetic. His letters, although not overly long, compress a lot of information into images. The tone is more businesslike than that of his poetry. Clearly, the texts of his works carry more weight for a critical analysis than his letters, which primarily tell us about Grotius the man of international affairs and an outstanding citizen of the world of letters.

The Poet-Scholar in Office (1601–18). Although Grotius occasionally wrote epigrams until 1644, and sent them to his brother Willem, by and large his poetic creativity lessened from 1608 on, the year he married Marie van Reigersbergh. Arthur Eijffinger found that of the 12,500 verses in *Poemata Collecta* less than 2,000 were written after 1609. Grotius reached his poetic peak during the years 1600–1603. During the first decade of the seventeenth century he laid the groundwork for his subsequent self-understanding. The States' Parallels opened his own eyes as to the possibilities of formulating legal principles and frame historical perspectives. His artistic and scientific interests blended well, but never interfered with his professional legal and administrative work. On the contrary, if anything, they enriched his experience and widened his intellectual capacities. Still Grotius as a ruling family's son neither made a living as an office-holder, for his family had other business interests,[7] nor as a writer.

Politically, his literary and scientific inclinations may not have been helpful to any extent. It is hard to see how he could fail to antagonize his opponents in government offices by the superior faculties of his mind and his thorough grasp of intellectual issues, as well as by his prodigious memory, from which he could quote widely and ad lib during his orations. Furthermore, it is no accident that his enemies could not defeat him by the force of written Dutch criminal and constitutional law. For he was brought down by arguments emanating from the unwritten law, as Fockema Andreae clearly shows.[8] Although he was by all accounts a brilliant public speaker, we do not know of any diehard political adherents. Apparently Grotius did not ever become too friendly with anybody. He became the head of a political party, the

Remonstrant or Toleration party, but as alter ego of the aging Oldenbarnevelt and not by achieving party control on his own. In our opinion, he was essentially an amateur politician by day and a professional scholar by night. Shortly before he was detained, his health broke down.

Humanist in Exile: His *Defense* (1621–34). Significantly, our humanist in exile wrote a defense of his reputation and of the legality of his political conduct in Dutch and finished it barely a year after his escape from Loevestein. His own translation also was achieved later in 1622. But interestingly, both defenses "lack the structural perfection and stylistic elegance which characterize the *Introduction* and the *Law of Prize*."[9]

Several of his friends admonished him not to publish this *Defense,* fearing for him that it would revive old animosities and not improve his chances for a return to Holland. He would not listen to their advice. Grotius instead obtained the privilege of the French King to print his *Apologeticus.* A Dutch decree was not long in appearing, declaring the work a seditious libel and outlawing the author, an underhanded invitation to some rogue to kill him. There appears to be an inverse relationship between the rigor of his sentence of 1619 and the tenor of his defense of 1622. Whereas the sentence somewhat overstressed his mere political guilt into a trumped-up charge of a crime close to high treason, constructed later as *laesa mejestas* by supplementary judgment, the written defense, which he was denied during the trial, completely whitewashes any implication whatsoever. Whereas Grotius as unsuccessful politician had no more than upset the unwritten constitutional balance, he now tried to tie the confederate character of the States of Holland with his loyal Hollandic service to his employer. The sentence fell short in respect to its legality, but the ex-post-facto apology defended somebody other than the accused. Grotius defended the lawful conduct of his government, not the nonsubversive character of his own policy. Procedurally, the prosecution was in the wrong from beginning to end, hence the sentence cannot have been totally legal.[10] But it was after all an extraordinary lawsuit, which was set into motion by the defender of the public faith who was also the commander-in-chief, Prince Maurits, under revolutionary circumstances, with the connivance of the States General. The legal character of the alleged crime, committed against a pseudomonarchical government, in essence consisted of secession from the Union *(imperium in imperio)* in respect to the militia's and the church governance's independence, and hence absence, from interference from below. In accordance with Roman common law, political conduct bordering on high treason could be punished by death or lifelong imprisonment under Dutch law. Precedents were not difficult to obtain, but they were not sought.

As a former attorney general Grotius had to be familiar with the likely outcome of his trial. We think J. Den Tex is justified in correcting the thesis that Oldenbarnevelt and Grotius were victims of "judicial murder."[11] Still, it has also been established that their criminal intent could not be proven during the trial either. Hence, subjectively and naively, the two politicians were innocent, but objectively and categorically, from the point of view of state reason, revolutionary as it might have been at that time, the supreme law of the land demanded their condemnation nevertheless. That is to say, the Land's Advocate and his Lieutenant were tragically implicated public figures, but so was their accuser, Maurits, who tried to uphold his oath of office sworn in 1584, in his own fashion. The High Court was driven by the intent,[12] at least, to serve justice, which was objectively a most difficult task, and thereby restore political unity. The Court failed procedurally, for seventeenth-century political criminal law suffered from imperfect standards. The trial itself is not a glorious leaf in the annals of Dutch constitutional law. An excess of zeal to protect the Union struck at the two honorable paladins of politically misguided tolerance. Who can judge the degree of turbulence in the eye of a storm?

The Diplomat for Christ's Reign (1635–45). For the sake of our summary it is important to perceive that Grotius never wavered in his allegiance to state and church, sovereign and friends. Rather he deepened it in the course of his life, if that course was left open to him. He entered Swedish foreign service for he thought that his diplomacy would benefit the Protestants' cause. He worked intellectually for gaining peace between the warring factions, and in a scholarly manner for gaining peace between the Christian confessions. Both tasks were interrelated to him. "The celestial fire"[13] in him increased in intensity throughout his life. He tried to reconcile "Nile" and "Jordan," "aberrant" and "true" religion, and critically worked through both Testaments for the ideal goal of reconciling Protestants and Catholics.

Diplomatically he suggested to Oxenstierna a split between two negotiating sites which ultimately fell on the Westphalian cities Osnabrück and Münster.[14] Symbolically both cities were neutralized, and tied territorially into one site of Christendom finding peace within itself. At the loss of personal comfort, the Swedish-Dutch diplomat worked both for the intellectual underpinning of peace as well as for its monetary realization, and he was successful in both respects, more so than he realized in his own modesty. His self-criticism, that he was not a courtier, was justified, but it did not and does not take courtiers to achieve lasting peace.

Although Grotius tripped in the arena of ecclesiastic politics, he decidedly triumphed in peacemaking during the last decade of his life. His reputation as a diplomat for Christ's reign on earth will not diminish. If anything, it has been underrated. His minor shortcomings in the realm of righteousness were a small price to pay. Prince Maurits was thoroughly misguided in taking Grotius for a turning weather vane. Grotius was not shrewd in judging people, but he was ironhearted in steering a course he perceived to be right. The diplomacy for Christ on earth is not tied to human protocol.

A Summary of His Main Works. His main literary occupation filled four major areas: (1) poetic literature from 1598–1608; (2) juridical treatises from 1606–31; (3) artistic philological editions from 1597–1630; (4) historical and annotative critical works, including annotations to the Testaments, 1600–45. In the combined areas of law and history, the development starts with the *States' Parallels,* splits into one branch, *DJPraedae* and *DJBPacis,* and into a second one, *Antiquitate* and *Annales.* In the area of religion and divinity, the development points from the poetic departure with *Godsdienst* to the critically annotative *Veritate.* Accordingly, the main thrust in the first area deepens from initial material clarity to aesthetic beauty; in the second area from aesthetic beauty to scientific acumen. The main works from the various disciplines are thus interrelated in terms of deep structure. Therefore, we may summarize the following fundamental parallels in a synoptical view:

(1) 1601 *Adamus Exul*	(1) 1606 *DJPr*	(1) 1613 *Pietas Ordinum*
(2) 1608 *Christus Patiens*	(2) 1609 *MLib*	(2) 1617 *Satisfactio Christi*
(3) 1635 *Sophompaneas*	(3) 1625 *DJBP*	(3) 1642 *Pax Ecclesiastica*
(1–3) man's fall redeems mankind	(1–3) exemplary law remedies wrongs	(1–3) dutiful law heals evils

The main parallel topics of his fundamental work remain throughout: God and Christ; War and Peace; State and Church. The interrelationships are governed in all rubrics by Grotius's epicizing sin, dutifying atonement, and exemplifying salvation. The intensive study of this literary trinity is the strong bond[15] combining all of Grotian literature.

A Short Survey of His Influence on Divinity—Law—Jurisprudence—Letters

It cannot be the purpose of this study to write the *Rezeptionsgeschichte,* the history of Grotius's total reception. Knight wrote a little, and van Vollenhoven[16] more intensively about it, and Ter Meulen and Diermanse published a separate bibliography about seventeenth-century writing on Grotius.[17] Almost 500 items appeared during his own century alone, mostly in the Netherlands, Germany, and Britain.

As a figure persecuted by his own government, Grotius radiated the heroic optimism of the exile; thus we are not surprised to learn that his humanistic common-man ideal left its footprint on Prussian and on several noted American writers, above all on Jonathan Edwards (1703–1758) and on the "freedom of will" Calvinism of New England theology. Grotius's atonement theory influenced Horace Bushnell of Yale University.[18] It would be fair to assess Grotius's influence on the science of jurisprudence as having been the most thoroughgoing in Prussia and the United States. This influence spread via two separate lines. First, the German professor Samuel Pufendorf, who studied at Leiden in 1660, used DJBP as a textbook in his public lectures from the Grotius chair of international law at Heidelberg before he was called to Berlin. John Wise (1652–1725), Harvard class of 1673, knew it well, too, before he published *A Vindication of the Government of New England*

Critical Evaluation

Churches in 1717.[19] He says that he cut an unbeaten path, but in reality, as H. Welzel has shown,[20] he bases his principles of Congregationalist church governance on an analogy to corporations governed by law of nature. He excerpts heavily from Pufendorf's classic *De Jure Naturae et Gentium* (1672), which in turn is based on Grotius's system of law of nature.[21] John Wise from Massachusetts is no less than the father of American Congregational democracy based on Grotian law of nature. Wise's *Vindication* is an almost unknown forerunner of American democratic theory. The components of democratic rights proceeded to develop in the order from within the church government to state government, not the other way around, or, to put it another way, the congregation's church governance preceded popular state government in the United States. Wise called these the "principles of natural knowledge" and also spoke of "the moral, spiritual and eternal happiness of men." "The end of all good government is to cultivate humanity, and promote the happiness of all, and the good of every man in all his rights, his life, liberty, estate, honor, etc., without injury or abuse to any."[22] Plainly, the language of the Declaration of Independence is indebted directly to John Wise and indirectly to Pufendorf and Grotius, who had developed the underlying concept of "societal egotism" (*appetitus societatis*).

The other line of influence in the United States proceeds via Henry Wheaton (1785–1848), who wrote *History of the Law of Nations* in 1841. But he started to spread Grotius's fame in the United States with a Grotius Oration[23] in 1820. This line spreads all the way to the Hague Peace Conferences of 1899 and 1907, and has to do with international law of security against criminal war and with arbitration in disputes between nations. Woodrow Wilson could be called a representative figure of this spirit, which, translated into peace policy, finally leads to the Nuremberg Nazi trials in 1946. "The picture what law is and of what the legal precepts should be, which is the background of judicial interpretation and application of due process of law, is largely Grotian."[24] Thus in hindsight Grotius ironically is admired as a most conservative revolutionary. His is the spirit of the reformed Christian's revolt against dogmatic dryness. He cannot of course be made to reappear as a latter-day shining knight, curing all legal ills of several epochs at once.[25]

More important (and most underrated) is his imprint on letters. To mention just his first biblical drama of epic dimensions, how dependent Milton's *Paradise Lost* really is on *Adamus Exul* has not yet been demonstrated.[26] We are only well informed of the relationship established between *Adamus Exul* and Vondel's *Adam in Ballingschap* (1664), and between *Sophompaneas* (1635) and Vondel's translation *Iosef of Sofompaneas* of the same year.[27] But Grotius's total influence as a "biblical humanist"[28] has not been fully researched as yet. This biblically based humanism is of the essence in judging his legal impact in the area of the law of nature and the law of nations as well.

Before a critical edition of Grotius's poetry has been completed, a view on how widely his lyrical poetry was adapted and imitated is premature. We only know a little of the use the German baroque poet Martin Opitz made of it.[29] In the first decade of the seventeenth century, Grotius and Daniel Heinsius cooperated closely. The knowledge of how Grotius's historical writing was used by subsequent Dutch historians and chroniclers must remain only partial until a critical edition of his main historical work, *Annales et Historiae,* becomes available.

We are on firmest ground if we cast a final glance at the influence of Grotius's writings on law and jurisprudence, which has been well researched ever since 1645. It is known that his *Inleidinghe* founded the discipline of Roman-Dutch law in South Africa, where his book had legal standing from 1859–1901, and that legal concepts created by Grotius were taken up and used by the *Nederlandsche Juristen-Vereeniging,* a law-drafting commission, in 1912. Grotius is generally credited with having founded a new theory of promise and a theory of property,[30] to name but two outstanding legal concepts of many.

The climactic characterization by the Italian philosopher G. Vico (1668–1744), who called Hugo Grotius "the jurisconsult of mankind"[31] in 1720, is not an overgenerous compliment, but an apt description of what Grotius achieved in the areas of his main work. And this judgment carries validity even today. Grotius applied all the faculties of his erudite mind to combat injustice of nature, which threatened people of all ages, and atoned for mankind by working abroad in the spirit of Christian understanding.

Critical Evaluation

Hugo Grotius could write equally well in elegant, classically oriented Latin, as could Huigh de Groot in powerfully rhythmical Dutch. Had he not been banished, he probably would have switched from Latin to Dutch permanently in the third decade of the seventeenth century, as Heinsius and the other leading Dutch writers of that time did. Grotius's Latin is, as we said, classical in manner. His Dutch, on the other hand, is creative and innovative. It has barely been researched. His Dutch encompasses lyrics, rhythmical prose, and powerful as well as elegant legal style. He was one of those truly bilingual writers the Netherlands brought forth in their Golden Age. Of the other great Dutch writers of his time none surpassed him in his Latin power of expression, and few, like Heinsius, were his equal in Dutch style. But who else tackled such fundamentally important topics, many of which still attract interest? In the realm of bilingual literature this great Hollander remained unsurpassed in his own time and remains unmatched concerning his living fame today. Furthermore, he proved to be far more influential, more lasting, than any of his enemies or friends. Although he failed as a Dutch statesman, perhaps due to unique bilingual thought processes not shared to the same degree by others, his works more than his life bear witness to his intellectual rank. Hugo Grotius's literary works ultimately were written for mankind.

Notes and References

Preface

1. So Reinder P. Meijer, *Literature of the Low Countries,* p. 107.
2. G. A. van Es and G. S. Overdiep, *Geschiedenis van de Letterkunde der Nederlanden,* in 9 volumes (Brussels/Den Bosch, 1947–51), 4:1–459.
3. In this parallelization Agamemnon represents Prince Maurits. This dramatization constitutes the source for an uninterrupted pro-Remonstrant tradition, argued for last by the Remonstrant-leaning H. Gerlach in his dissertation of 1965 (see summary and notes to Chapter 6). We ourselves were a convinced adherent of this undifferentiating myth until 1979.

Chapter One

1. See Primary Sources, TMD 411, in the Bibliography. Since the young man was out of the country, a sketch by de Gheyn of 1590 was reused for convenience; more than eight years had passed from that sitting. The edition in question appeared a day before his sixteenth birthday. Beresteyn, plate 2, shows a "childlike" H. G. because he was only seven, not fifteen, as alleged by everybody. On plate 4, he is shown as he really looked at sixteen, masculine, bright, and handsome. All the famous prints, showing him with the medallion, are thus print montages only. This is most likely true of other contemporary Grotius prints, too. The portrait we chose for our frontispiece shows a contemporary Grotius of 1613–14 as a thirty-year-old. It is connected to an authentic text of 1614 and is not a montage. We chose it carefully from the extensive *Porträtarchiv Diepenbroick, Westfälisches Landesmuseum für Kunst und Kulturgeschichte Münster,* with whose kind permission Grotius's portrait is reproduced.
2. He could be appointed Royal Swedish Court Bibliographer and/or State Counsellor. After his refusal Grotius received 12,000 Riksdalers as equivalent for arrears in salary.

Chapter Two

1. A. Eijffinger, *Forum der Letteren* (1978), p. 223.
2. A word-for-word rhymed translation into English would sound staccato. For such a versified translation see Watson Kirkconnell, *The Celestial Cycle* (New York: Gordian Press, 1967), pp. 96–220, 583–85.

3. The play was probably presented to the French Court in 1602, with Prince Henri Condé, to whom *Adamus Exul* was dedicated, present.

4. Meulenbroek, *De Dichtwerken,* (1970), I:1A:184–87.

5. E H. Bodkin, *Grotiana* (1931), 4:24; Meulenbroek, *De Dichtwerken* (1971), I:1B/21; Eijffinger, *De Dichtwerken* (1978), I:2A/B5:31.

6. First noted by H. Bekker, *Neophilologus* (1969), 44:239.

7. Kirkconnell translates "peace pact" mistakenly as "eternal faith" (149); see also v. 928: "let's rule as one."

8. In his next drama, *Christus Patiens* (1608), the same charge is leveled against Christ by His own people, v. 680.

9. Genesis 2:24 and Matthew 19:5.

10. Genesis 1:29–30 and 9:2.

11. For Grotius's subsequently developed theory of the origin of property *(proprietatis exordium)* see *De Jure Belli ac Pacis* Book II 2 § 1–2 and our Chapter 5.

12. Discussed by Meulenbroek in greater detail, *De Dichtwerken,* (1971), Notes to *Adamus Exul,* I:1B:70–71.

13. Kirkconnell misses this point on p. 189.

14. Compare John 8:44. For further details see Chapter 5.

15. See v. 1307–8. Joost van den Vondel (1587–1679) called his own version, *Adam in Ballingschap,* "the tragedy of all tragedies" in his subtitle.

16. Kirkconnell translates this passage into "the use of reason," but Man cannot be said to command "the use of reason" before eating from the Tree.

17. *De Jure Belli ac Pacis* Book II § 11, 4, 1.

18. See *De Dichtwerken,* I:1B:33.

19. This precarious point of view is corrected by Grotius in *Christus Patiens* (1608).

20. Molhuysen, *BW,* I, no. 463.

21. Eijffinger, "De Dichter H.G.," p. 24; documented in his unpublished "inventaris van de latijnse poezie van hugo grotius" (1980), p. 78.

22. *BW,* no. 1912, 5:231.

23. This error is expressed by Hans K. E. L. Keller, *Hugo Grotius: Ein Passionsspiel* (Munich: n.p., 1959), 137 pp.

24. "Ter Inleiding," in *De Dichtwerken* (1978), 2A:5:23–36. This Introduction contains helpful hints about how to read *Christus Patiens.*

25. Andrew D. Weiner, *Sir Philip Sidney and the Poetics of Protestantism: A Study of Contexts* (Minneapolis: University of Minnesota Press, 1978), p. 24.

26. Eijffinger, "Ter Inleiding," pp. 23, 26.

Notes and References

27. Paul Stachel, *Seneca und das deutsche Renaissancedrama. Palaestra* (1907; rpt. 1967), 46:158.
28. This point will be enlarged upon later in this chapter.
29. We consider this passage, *ruit in exitum meum ferale tempus* (74–75): *"ruit . . . tempus"* as the poetical underpinning of Hugo Grotius's emblematic *"ruit hora"* motto. His literary source is very probably Ti. Silius Italicus, *Punica,* 6:364–66, plus the image used by Seneca, *Hercules Furens,* 840–42.
30. Here Seneca's belief in Fatalism and the Calvinistic belief in Predestination fuse; see Stachel, p. 160. Hence, it would be difficult to determine whether Grotius wrote his play as a convinced "infralapsarian," as he was later on, when he published his *Pietas* in 1613; see Chapter 5, note 11.
31. The quotation is from a letter to Grotius's brother Willem, *BW* I, no. 441.
32. *BW* V, no. 1912.
33. Gerhard von Rad, *Das erste Buch Mose. Das Alte Testament Deutsch* (Göttingen: Neues Göttinger Bibelwerk, 1972), 2/4:356.
34. The Grotius Institute in The Hague plans to issue this critical edition by the end of the 1980s.
35. We use the first edition of 1635.
36. In his first edition Grotius makes Joseph's exile last fifteen years; in TMD 153, issued half a year later, he wanted it changed to twenty-two years. See letter to Vossius, dated 17 February 1634, *BW* V, no. 1914. See also below.
37. L. Strengholt, *Vondel: Joseph in Dothan: Treurspel,* 4th ed. (1974), p. 12. See also Chapter 6.
38. Letter to his brother Willem, dated 6 June 1643: *"Poetica[m] . . . peculiarum laude nostrae familiae . . ." Epistolae,* Appendix no. 656.
39. S. F. Witstein, *Funeraire Poëzie in de Nederlandse Renaissance. Neerlandica Traiectina,* no. 17, 1969, pp. 355–58.
40. See G. Ellinger, *Geschichte der Neulateinischen Lyrik in den Niederlanden* (1933), 3:1:204.
41. Daniel Heinsius (1580–1655) was appointed to this post in 1627.
42. Bodkin, "The Minor Poetry of Hugo Grotius," *Transactions of the Grotius Society* (London, 1928), 13:106.
43. In real life Grotius became legal counsellor to Prince Maurits.
44. Both *Poemata Collecta,* 1st ed. (1616) and 2d ed. (1639), wrongly identify the year in question as 1612, when Grotius neither turned thirty nor spent time in London.
45. See Chapter 1 for further clarification.
46. Bodkin, "Minor Poetry," p. 105.

47. The fishing rights question stayed unsolved and the theological points of differences could not be bridged either.

48. His yearly salary at that time amounted to 2,000 guilders, which was twice the sum a seafaring captain earned at that time.

49. His father, Jan de Groot, upheld this poetic family tradition by writing Hugo a birthday poem for 1615. He alludes to the fact that Hugo's son, Pieter I, died as an infant in 1614, and that Pieter II was born in March 1615 (*"pia gaudia luctu,"* v. 11–12).

50. The first one, *"Plaudite Mauritio victori,"* of 1591, was published when Hugo-Jan (= Hugeianus), as he called himself in honor of his father until his return from France in 1599, was just eight.

51. For a brief discussion of Aratos's *Constellations* see Chapter 3.

52. As demonstrated by Eijffinger, "Prent en Puntdicht (Grotius' Maurits-Epigrammen)," *Oud-Holland* 92 (1978):161–206.

53. Under Simon Stevin's and Rudolf Snellius's tutelage the Prince had developed into a first-rate arithmetician and ballistic/hydraulic expert at the University of Leiden. When his father was murdered, he could not continue his studies for a degree.

54. *Oldenbarnevelt* (The Hague, 1937; 3rd ed., 1953) last page, 202. For a more differentiating assessment of Barnevelt's relation to Grotius see Den Tex, discussed in Chapter 6.

55. H. C. Rogge, *Brieven van en aan Maria van Reigersbergh* (Leiden: Brill, 1902), 340 pp.; Robert Fruin, *Allerliefste van Hugo de Groot,* Ooievaar. 58 (The Hague, 1957), 176 pp.

56. Vv. 97–110 of "Silva ad Thuanum" (*"Certa patris"*), 357 vv., taken and translated from *Poemata Collecta,* 2d ed. (1639), pp. 524–35.

57. The translation, particularly of line 8 of this poem, by Judge W. J. M. van Eysinga in *Huigh de Groot* (1945), p. 15, misses the point of this epigram: *Peccet necesse est saepe, qui numquam negat* ("Diegeen moet noodzakelijkerwijze dikwijls mistasten, die nooit neen kan zeggen" = "He who can never say no, of necessity must often go wrong"). The epigram clearly deals with the ethics of the lawyer's profession. See Chapter 6.

58. Line 16, the punch line of this poem, is given a misinterpretation in *Anthologia Grotiana* (1955), pp. 38–39: "Not to know certain matters is the main business of wisdom!" Grotius is playing on the stoic paradox, "I know that I do not know!" The translator failed to connect the juxtaposed *quaedam* with *sapientia*.

59. We therefore suppose that this poem belongs in the orbit of Grotius's posthumously published Collection on Fate (= *Philosophorum sententiae de fato et de eo quod in nostra est potestate,* TMD 523); see Chapter 3.

60. According to Eijffinger's inventory *PC,* 2d ed. (1639) lists all 290 epigrams which had appeared in *PC,* 1st ed. (1616) again.

61. For an introduction consult Gerald O. McCulloh, ed., *Man's Faith and Freedom: The Theological Influence of Jacobus Arminius* (New York: Nashville, 1962); see Chapter 5.

62. In *Poemata Collecta,* 1st ed. (1616), pp. 435–52; *PC,* 2d ed. (1939), pp. 370–88. *De Dichtwerken* (1977), I:2A:2:16–49 and (1977), I:2B:2:15–59; on the dating, see ibid., p. 16. Meulenbroek is opting for 1597; Eijffinger, "inventaris," p. 43, for 1600. See Grotius's own inconclusive dating in *De Dichtwerken* (1970), I:1A:295. See also note 65.

63. Compiled for the Emperor Justinian in A.D. 533. See R. Sohm-L. Mitteis-L. Wenger, *Institutionen: Geschichte und System des Römischen Privatrechts,* 17th ed. (Berlin: Duncker & Humblot, 1928), Chapter 5, p. 2.

64. In his *Poemata Collecta.* Letter to coeditor Vossius dated 17 July 1616, *BW* I, no. 463. In his *Index poematum* Grotius refers to his paraphrase as "song" *(carmen).*

65. We also detect a satirical proximity to Grotius's 1599 edition of Martianus Capella's *The Seven Liberal Arts;* see Chapter 3.

66. Robert Feenstra, "Der Eigentumsbegriff bei Hugo Grotius," in *Festschrift für Franz Wieacker* (Göttingen, 1978), p. 226.

67. Discussed in Chapter 5.

68. Grotius's autograph *klad* manuscript MS Papenbroeck 10, encompasses his poetic production of 1601–9. A comparison shows that one-third of that poetic output was not elevated into *PC,* 1st ed. (1616).

69. These statistics are based on Arthur Eijffinger's "inventaris." Grotius's poetry was put on the list of Prohibited Books by the Spanish Inquisition; see TMD 1, note 6.

70. That the *Bewijs* expressed "part of his pain" is indicated in his letter to Cl. Sarravius dated 5 March 1640, *Epistolae* (Amsterdam, 1687), no. 1331.

71. Their initials are dissolved by Ter Meulen-Diermanse in TMD 215 note 1, p. 85.

72. Titled *Hugo de Groot's Bewijs van de ware godsdienst, met zijne overige Nederduitsche gedichten* (Amsterdam: R. Stemvers, 1844), pp. 286–89. Hallema, *Prins Maurits,* does not seem to doubt this poem's authenticity, but he does not date it. We would have to date the poem sometime before December 1599, when Grotius was admitted to the bar.

73. Hallema identifies the "Lady of Mechelen" as Margaretha van Mechelen, who bore Prince Maurits three sons out of wedlock.

74. Meulenbroek, *BW* IV (1964), no. 1571.

75. S. J. Fockema Andreae, *Inleiding tot de Hollandsche Rechts-Geleertheyd,* 2d ed. (Leiden, 1910), XIII. See below, Chapter 5.

76. *Parallelon Rerum Publicarum.* Liber Tertius, chapter XXV De lingua, pp. 54–73; TMD 750, note 6, gives the dating. See Chapter 4.

77. Grotius translated Stevin's *Limenheuretica,* a kind of Nautical Pathfinder, in 1599.

78. See Simon Stevin, *Het Burgerlijk Leven* (of Leiden, 1590), newly edited by G. S. Overdiep (Amsterdam: Wereldbibliotheek, 1939). See *The Principal Works of Simon Stevin,* 6 volumes (Amsterdam, 1955–66).

79. Five years before the appearance of the *Bewijs* the Dutch Merchant Marine had large crews of seamen. See *Maritieme Geschiedenis der Nederlanden* (Bussum, 1977), 2:130.

80. Following Rogge 350 rather than Ter Meulen-Diermanse, TMD 144. We believe that TMD 143 was printed in second place during the same year. TMD 143 was printed in a hurry, and consequently has printing errors to correct.

81. See Grotius's Project of an Order concerning the treatment of the Jews in Holland of 1615 (TMD 816).

82. See TMD 143 ff. for the Dutch versions, and 944 ff. for the Latin versions.

83. We adapted some points of our interpretation from Cornelia W. Roldanus, *Bewys van den waren Godsdienst* (Arnhem, 1944).

84. The contents of Book I are also found condensed into *DJBP* II 20 § 45–46.

Chapter Three

1. TMD 411 ff.

2. William Harris Stahl, Richard Johnson, and E. L. Burge, eds., *Martianus Capella and the Seven Liberal Arts.* Records of Civilization, no. 8, vol. 1 (New York: Columbia University Press, 1971), p. 178; vol. 2 appeared in 1977.

3. Eleanor Shipley Duckett, *Latin Writers of the Fifth Century* (n.p.: Archon Books, 1969), pp. 224–34.

4. Duckett, *Latin,* p. 232; Wessner, *Pauly-Wissowa's Real-Encyclopädie der Classischen Altertumswissenschaft* (1928–30), 14:col. 2003–16.

5. Only space limitations preclude looking further into Grotius's cooperation with Simon Stevin's main scientific work; see TMD 407–10 and Chapter 2, note 78.

6. See Chapter 5.

7. *BW* II, no. 930, dated 8 November 1624, p. 409: "But that I

should take upon myself the professor's burden, would hardly amount to great honors."

8. See Harm Wansink, *Political Science at Leyden University 1575–1650* (Utrecht: Proefschrift, 1975); tr. into English.

9. Duckett, *Latin,* p. 233.

10. TMD, no. 411, note 10. Index Librorum Prohibitorum, Ter Meulen-Diermanse, *Bibliographie des Ecrits sur Hugo Grotius imprimées au XVIIe siècle* (1961), pp. 184–92.

11. This was the popular title. Grotius changed it to "Syntagma Arateorum" = Constellations; see TMD 411 ff.

12. E.g., G. R. Mair, *Kallimachus/Aratus. Loeb Classical Library.* no. 129 (New York, 1921; rpt 1960).

13. W. Ludwig, "Aratos," Pauly-Wissowa, *Realencyclopädie der Classischen Altertumswissenschaft.* Supplementary vol. 10 (Stuttgart, 1965), pp. 26–39.

14. *Hermes* 91 (1963):447 and note 4.

15. D. B. Gain, *The Aratus Ascribed to Germanicus Caesar* (London: Athlone of London Press, 1976).

16. "De Platen in de Aratea van Hugo de Groot," *Mededeelingen der Koninklijke Nederlandsche Akademie van Wetenschappen, afd. letterkunde.* N.R. 12,2 (1949) 169–235.

17. Before the appearance of the definitive work on the de Gheyns by J. Q. v. Regteren Altena with Sijthoff and Noordhoff we cannot comment on Grotius's poems on the engravings.

18. TMD 413, note 8; see also 352.

19. See *Grotiana* (1940) 8:30–31.

20. See C. Wachsmuth, *Joannis Stobaei Anthologii libri priores et posteriores,* 1–4 (1884; rpt. Berlin: Weidmann, 1958).

21. *BW* II letter 2 February 1620, p. 28.

22. See TMD 458–67.

23. The three Greek philosophers are also the ones most frequently alluded to in *De Jure Belli ac Pacis* (1625).

24. *Excerpts from Greek Tragedies and Comedies* (Paris, 1626) = TMD 468.

25. The nucleus of this study appeared as an appendix to Heinsius's edition of Aristotle's Poetics (1610–11) *("De tragica constitutione liber"),* and separately as *De tragoediae constitutione liber. Editio auctor multo* (Leiden, 1643). We consulted the erudite study by J. H. Meter, *De Literaire Theorieën van Daniel Heinsius* (Amsterdam: Hakkert, 1975), 646 pp.; and the highly informative Twayne study *Daniel Heinsius* by Baerbel Becker-Cantarino (1979).

26. Meter, *Literaire,* p. 606.
27. *Poetics,* 13.
28. *De Constitutione Tragoediae,* IV § 9; Meter, *Literaire,* p. 549–50.
29. The adaptor into Dutch, Vondel, titles his version accordingly, *Gebroeders* = Brethren of Thebes.
30. See TMD 534, note 8; Lubinus is not mentioned by TMD 534–37.
31. *Philosophorum Sententiae de Fato* (Paris, 1648), published by Marie v. Reigersbergh; see TMD 523. We used the TMD 524 Amsterdam edition of the same year.
32. J. L. Saunders, *Justus Lipsius: The Philosophy of Renaissance Stoicism* (New York, 1955); and R. H. Popkin, *The History of Scepticism from Erasmus to Descartes.* See also note 46.
33. Chr. Jöcher, *Allgemeines Gelehrten-Lexicon* (Leipzig, 1750), col. 1205.
34. See Chapter 2.
35. J. D. Duff, *Lucanus' Pharsalia. The Loeb Classical Library* 220 (Harvard, 1928; Rpt., 1969). We used Grotius's 1643 ed. = TMD 430.
36. See Chapter 3.
37. On Book III see especially M. P. O. Morford, *The Poet Lucan* (Oxford, 1967), p. 50.
38. See Erich Burck, "Das Menschenbild in Lucans Pharsalia," in *Wege der Forschung* (Darmstadt, 1970), 235:145 ff.
39. Freely paraphrased from Book VII, 207–13.
40. E. L. Etter, *Tacitus in der Geistesgeschichte des 16. und 17. Jahrhunderts.* Diss., Basel, 1966. pp. 115–48. See also H. Wansink, *Politieke Wetenschappen aan de Leidse Universiteit,* Diss., Utrecht, 1975, pp. 106–40.
41. E.g., by Daniel Heinsius, *Politieke,* p. 140.
42. Contrary to the Dutch preference for Civilis's attitude, the Germans admired and officially revered, until 1945, Arminius the Cheruscan, abhorred by Grotius.
43. TMD 741, note 3.
44. See Mulders's adapted etchings in P. C. Hooft, *Alle de Werken van C. Corn. Tacitus In't Hollandsch vertaalt* (1684) (Amsterdam/Leiden/Utrecht, 1704). Grotius's own forefathers named De Cornet were from Burgundy.
45. The latter costumes are imitations of Philipp Cluverius, *De Germania Antiqua* (Leiden, 1616).
46. Etter, p. 159, note 285; Gerhard Oestreich, "J. Lipsius als Theoretiker des neuzeitlichen Machtstaates," in *Geist und Gestalt des frühmodernen Staates,* p. 75.
47. We refer to TMD 515; see M. Hutton *Tacitus Germania. Loeb Classical Library* (rpt. 1963).

Notes and References

48. Brandt-Cattenburgh, *Het Leven van H. de Groot* (1727), 1:183.
49. A. H. Haentjens, *H. de Groot als Godsdienstig Denker* (1946), p. 32, erroneously reports that the second part of the Annotations to the Old Testament appeared in 1646.
50. Franz H. Reusch, *Der Index der verbotenen Bücher* (Bonn: Cohen, 1885), 2:1:102–6. Only in 1757 were his *Opera Omnia Theologica* (Amsterdam and London, 1679), TMD 919–20, indexed under Pope Benedict XIV.
51. The German reeditors G. I. L. Vogel and C. Döderlein (Halle, 1776) list about 450 named subscribers.
52. Epist. no. 1396, p. 636. Grotius must have been familiar with the Dordrecht Bible (1637) of the Reformed Church.
53. C. W. Roldanus, Review of Haentjens's book, *De Gids* (1941), 110:140.
54. TMD 1157 in 3 vols.
55. A comment on the fourth book of Maccabees, which is stoic, curiously is missing.
56. Emanuel Hirsch, *Geschichte der neueren evangelischen Theologie im Zusammenhang mit den allgemeinen Bewegungen des europäischen Denkens* (Gütersloh: Mohn, 5th ed., 1975), 1:18.
57. Ibid., p. 226.
58. Haentjens, *Hugo de Groot*, pp. 27–30. "Rationalism" for Grotius was God-given.
59. *De Jure Belli ac Pacis* (ed. Molhuysen 1919) Prolegomena 51.
60. Votum pro pace ecclesiastica, *Opera Omnia Theologica* (1679) 3:672. See Chapter 5.
61. Haentjens, *Hugo de Groot*, pp. 31–35.
62. The allegorical, typological, tropological, and anagogical sense.
63. *Huigh de Groot*, p. 132: *"een stuk Wereldlitteratuur."*
64. E.g., in Isaiah 9:6, 61:1; Jeremiah 23:4; Hosea 11:1; Zachariah 4:6.
65. We follow Haentjens's judgment here, pp. 36 ff. Knight, *The Life and Works of Hugo Grotius*, gives no evidence for his opinion that Grotius "was only to a limited extent a believer in inspiration and revelation" (257).
66. Haentjens, p. 39; corroborated by A. Borst, *Der Turmbau von Babel* (Stuttgart, 1960) 3:1298–99.
67. For English translation and spelling we adhere to *The New Oxford Annotated Bible with Apocrypha: Revised Standard Version* (New York: Oxford University Press, 1977).
68. DJBP I, 1 § 15 & Prolegomena.
69. Haentjens aptly translates into Dutch, "poetische minnezang," *Hugo de Groot*, p. 41.

70. Further examples can be gathered from Haentjens, *Hugo de Groot,* pp. 41–44.

71. *"Justitia est constans & perpetua voluntas,"* Ad Librum I Institutionum, H.G. *Florum Sparsio ad Jus Justinianeum,* ed. G. C. Gebauer (Naples, 1777), p. 5 = TMD 795. In a letter to Willem de Groot, Ep. 534 App. 915, he speaks of an immovable sense of the gospels.

72. Emanuel Hirsch, *Geschichte der neuern Evangelischen Theologie,* I p., 5th ed., 1975, pp. 225–30. Haentjens, *Hugo de Groot,* p. 54 ff., 46 ff.

73. Hirsch, *Geschichte,* p. 228.

74. *DJBP* I, 1 § 15.

75. Haentjens, *Hugo de Groot,* p. 89; J. Schlüter, *Die Theologie des H.G.,* p. 36.

76. Separately published as *Annotationes ad Sermonem Christi in monte habitam* in the seventeenth and eighteenth centuries. Theodor Zahn, *Das Evangelium des Matthäus.* Leipzig, 3rd ed., 1910, lists only two seventeenth-century commentaries on M. as relevant in the twentieth; the one is by Grotius.

77. Haentjens, *Hugo de Groot,* p. 48.

78. See *DJBP* I, 1 § 6; II, 1 § 13.

79. *The New Oxford Annotated Bible* (1977) footnotes this sentence.

80. Hammond is the second annotator listed by editor John Lindsay, *The New Testament of Our Lord and Saviour Jesus Christ,* in 2 vols. (London: R. Penny, 1736) = TMD 1164.

81. See the sixty-four anti-Grotian "Caloviana" containing the names and works of no fewer than eighty respondents in TMD, *Bibliographie des écrits sur Hugo Grotius* (1961), pp. 159–83.

82. We are not sure whether an adequate history of the Reformed Church Research-History has been written.

83. *Geschichte,* pp. 227–29.

84. Leopold von Ranke, *Die Römischen Päpste* (Vienna, 1934), p. 614. It is the Pope who had Galileo condemned.

85. In our view, Dr. Knight's *The Life and Works of Hugo Grotius,* although published in 1925, bases its scholarship on secondary sources of the nineteenth century and is therefore outdated in many respects. See Karl Barth, *Die Kirchliche Dogmatik I, 2. Die Lehre vom Wort Gottes,* 2d ed. (Zurich: Zollikon, 1969), p. 617.

86. Ep. 534 App. p. 914, letter to his brother Willem dated 1641.

Chapter Four

1. W. Fikentscher, *De Fide et perfidia,* 1979, advanced our knowledge considerably. Fikentscher, *Methoden des Rechts in vergleichender Darstellung*

Notes and References

(Tübingen, 1975–77), 5 vols., Grotian in scope, learnedness, and in spirit, was very helpful for our booklet on Grotius.

2. See R. Fruin, W. van Eysinga, G. S. Overdiep, H. Kampinga, P. Diermanse, TMD 750, notes 5, 6.

3. The parallels do not deal with the Dutch "Renaissance" as Overdiep, *Onze Renaissance in Proza,* Wereldbibliotheek 700 (1939), alleges, p. 9.

4. A. Stempels, "Ter Inleiding," in *Hugo de Groot: Over Goede Trouw en onbetrouwbaarheid* (The Hague: Boucher, 1945), p. 7.

5. Is the frame of 26 units supposed to remind one of Plutarch's *Parallel Lives?*

6. See Cicero, *De Officio,* and Lipsius, *De Constantia* (1585); *Politicorum sive civilis doctrina* (1590).

7. Wansink, "Historia magistra vitae," *Politieke Wetenschappen,* pp. 66 ff.

8. W. Dilthey, *Gesammelte Schriften* (1892; 8th ed. 1969), 2:91.

9. Grotius decides in favor of Laurensz Janszoon Coster (1405–1484) from Haarlem as having invented the movable metal letter type. Coster used sand-cast channels for casting letters of low-resistant and poor printing quality for short schoolbooks before Gutenberg.

10. *Fide et Perfidia,* p. 49 ff.

11. *Dogmatischer Teil* (1977), 4:69–71.

12. The *civilis scientia* is translated "Staatswetenschap" by Meulenbroek, and identified as Ciceronian-Quintilian; see *Dichtwerken* I:1A:296–97; I:1B:202.

13. Quoted as "a book" already in 1601; compare the afterword on his *Sacra* to the text; the reference is not, as Meulenbroek I:1B:202 alleges, to the *Annales.* See below.

14. G. S. Overdiep-Annie Romein-Verschoor, ed.; *Stichting Onze Oude Letteren* (Amsterdam, 1939), 63 pp.

15. A summary of Chapter 6 is given by Fikentscher, *Fide,* pp. 40–47.

16. Stempels, "Ter Inleiding," p. 33; *Fide,* p. 114.

17. Rpt. in part in G. J. de Voogd, *Erasmus en Grotius* (Leiden, w.y. 179 ff.).

18. Meerman, *Parallelon,* p. 32. Grotius was not a pacifist per se as was Erasmus.

19. Ibid., pp. 81, 109.

20. Edward Dumbauld, *The Life and Legal Writings of Hugo Grotius* (1969), p. 25.

21. Ironically Grotius translated Stevin in Latin; see TMD 407, in 1599.

22. *Het Burgherlicke Leven* [1590] (1939), p. 14.

23. Meerman, *Parallelon,* p. 64. George K. Zipf, *The Psycho-Biology of Language* (Cambridge, MIT Press, 1965).
24. Meerman, *Parallelon,* p. 101.
25. J. Lecler, *Geschichte der Religionsfreiheit,* vol. 2, Chapter 5, dealing with the question of tolerance in the Netherlands from 1580–1600.
26. Final sentence of Chapter 7.
27. Kampinga, *De Opvattingen over onze vaderlandsche Geschiedenis, etc.* (1917), p. 83.
28. Kampinga, *Opvattingen,* p. 74 ff. Grotius also knew of Bodin's *De Republica libri sex,* book 5, Chapter 1. See Plato, *The State,* Book IV § 11.
29. Check TMD 695, 72–73.
30. Which was not authorized for publication.
31. About the difficulties of that interpretation in respect to the *graafshap* Holland, see Kampinga, *Opvattingen,* p. 149 ff.
32. Originally written in Dutch (TMD 872), rewritten in Latin (TMD 880), but both published in 1622. Our edition (881) has 355 pp.
33. Fikentscher, *Methoden des Rechts,* 4:556–58.
34. *Methodus ad facilem historiarum cognitionem* (Paris, 1566), Chapter 4, "De recto historiarum judicio," ed. F. Renz (1905). Van Eysinga, *Huigh de Groot,* judges rather mildly about de Groot's historiography, p. 27.
35. I. H. Goosses and R. R. Post, eds., *De Middeleeuwen,* vol. I, 2d ed. (The Hague: Nijhoff, 1974), 300 pp.
36. According to a mimeographed paper on *werkzaamheden* issued by the Grotius Instituut in November 1976, p. 37, there will be no attempt made to undertake this editorial work.
37. *BW* I 314, 5 February 1614.
38. *BW* I 319, 299.
39. Italics and addition of year and footnote are mine.
40. *BW* I 409, 396.
41. See *Annales et Historiae,* TMD 735; both parts have roman-numbered chapters, quoted henceforth as A I–V and as H I–XVIII.
42. Eysinga, Meerman, and Fikentscher are in agreement here.
43. Beresteyn, *Iconographie,* plate 16 and p. 79. The epigram by Heinsius is reattached to an engraving by Mierevelt of 1631. This print-montage graces the principal edition of Grotius's *Annales et Historiae* (1657).
44. The translation by Brandt's father in *Leven van Hugo de Groot* (1727), p. 65, is misleading: *"Dit's pand van 's hemels gunst, van Hollandt voortgebragt, Dat zich met recht ontzette en by zich zelven dacht Heb ik dien grooten HUIG wel voor my zelfs gebaert? Dit zichtbaer menschlyk is, de rest naer't godlyk aert."* In our opinion, the construction has to be fully dissolved. See p. 92.
45. First Tim. 6:20; 2 Tim. 1:14; Sermon on the Mount, Matt. 6:19–21.

46. The term "instar" helps to date Heinsius's poem around October 1614.
47. *BW* I 187 162.
48. *BW* III 1087 60; ep. 1334 402.
49. *BW* VIII (1637) ep. 3373 772.
50. *TMD* 741 ed. (1657) 3 f.
51. Clifford H. Moore, ed., *Tacitus: The Histories,* 1–5 in 2 vols., *The Loeb Classic Library* (1962); see R. Hanslink, *Lustrum,* vols. 16 and 17 (Göttingen, 1974–76), on recent Tacitus research.
52. John Jackson, ed., *Tacitus: The Annals,* 1–6; 11–16 in 3 vols., *The Loeb Classical Library* (1962–63).
53. Each chapter of A and H is preceded by a half-page summary.
54. Henri C. A. Muller, *Hugo de Groots "Annales et Historiae"* (Utrecht: J. van Druten, 1919), 194 pp.
55. (a) *Oorsprongh, Beghin en Vervolgh der Nederlandsche Oorlogen (tot 1573)* in 6 vols., 1st ed. (1559); 2d ed. (1603); 3rd ed. (1621); (b) *Historie . . .* (1614); *Commentarien* (1608); (c) *Historie der Nederlantscher Oorlogen . . . tot 1601* (1626).
56. See Meulenbroek's extensive documentation in his editions of *De Dichtwerken van Hugo Grotius,* in Chapter 2.
57. Kampinga, *Opvattingen,* p. 199, accuses Grotius outright of tendentiousness *("strekkingen van politieken aard");* Muller, *H.d.G's Annales,* says that Grotius is following a utilitarian method, p. 24.
58. Cf. Aerschot's oratory, p. 204; oration to Elizabeth, p. 434; Admiral Heemskerk's address, p. 514; Jeanin's presentation to the States, p. 547; Breda, p. 139; Bergen-op-Zoom, p. 124; Groningen, p. 186; Cadiz, Spain, p. 256. These site descriptions are faded out in the latter part of H.
59. Cf. Henry Smith Williams, ed., *The Historians' History of the World,* in 25 volumes (New York/London, 1904).
60. Muller in his sixth chapter, pp. 163–86, decides that A and H are a work of art, rather than a scientific historical treatise.
61. E. L. Etter, *Tacitus in der Geistesgeschichte des 16. und 17. Jahrhunderts.* Diss., Basel, 1966, notes 212, 217.
62. *De Bello Gallico,* H VII 344. A careful observer would find several other allusions to Caesar's style. A & H was originally titled *Commentarii.*
63. See list by Muller, pp. 186–90. Cf. Chapter 5, note 122.
64. Tacitus, *Annales* 1:1.
65. Etter, *Tacitus i.d. Gg.,* 138–40; 11 ff. It needs to be noted, however, that Grotius does not employ a hiatus-less style, as pure "Atticists" do. Rather he says nov*i o*rbis; aegr*ee*s, e.g., p. 316—a random page picked.
66. A. Dihle, *Hermes* 85 (1957):170–205.

67. A modern summary on the revolt of the Netherlands is presented by Heinz Schilling, "Der Aufstand der Niederlande: Bürgerliche Revolution oder Elitenkonflikt?" *200 Jahre amerikanische Revolution und moderne Revolutionsforschung,* ed. H.-U. Wehler (Göttingen, 1976), pp. 177–231. The classic in this area is Pieter Geyl, *The Revolt of the Netherlands (1555– 1609),* 2d ed. (London: Benn, 1958).

68. S. J. Fockema Andreae, *Grotiana* 10 (1942–47):41.

69. *BW* VII ep. 2734 354–56. According to this letter, further legal sources *(Leges Barbarorum)* were cut out by L. Elzevier.

70. Leiden, 1595; enlarged by a section of Jordanes, Hamburg, 1611; 2d ed., Leiden, 1617. He also published a *Codex Legum Antiquarum.*

71. See note 69 and *BW* VIII (1637) 3132 369–71.

72. The letters dealing with this issue are quoted in TMD 735, note 7.

73. According to the title-of-works checklist of nearly 500 entries by Sellin, *Daniel Heinsius and Stuart England* (1968), H. left his Prokopius ed. in the planning stage; see ibid., p. 58.

74. *Grotiana* 10, p. 41.

75. For Prokopius's part see H. B. Dewing, *Prokopius. The Loeb Classical Library,* 7 vols. (Cambridge: Harvard University Press, 1961).

76. See R. G. van de Velde, *De Studie van het Gotisch in de Nederlanden* (Ghent: Kl. Vlaamse Academie, 1966), pp. 124–27.

77. Ed. 43–55.

78. J. Svennung, *Jordanes und Scandia: Kritisch-exegetische Studien* (Stockholm: Almquist & Wiksell, 1967); consult also Norbert Wagner, *Getica. Quellen und Forschungen.* New Series 22 (Berlin: de Gruyter, 1967).

79. Ed. 707.

80. We shall have to come back briefly to some legal-historical ramifications in Chapter 5.

Chapter Five

1. *States' Parallels,* Chapter XXVI, "About Religion and Piety"; see p. 69. The term *pietas* occurs only there on p. 73. He probably adapted the ecclesiastical meaning of the term from John Barclay's *Pietas . . . sive publicae pro regibus . . . vindiciae* (Paris, 1612), a copy of which was part of his library at that time, item 140 of Molhuysen's list, *MNAW* (1943), 6:3:12, rather than directly from Th. Erastes' *Explicatio* (1589). Barclay's notion of piety is usually referred to as "royal Gallicanism" and argues for a control of royal lawyers over church government.

2. Uitenbogaert is not named on the title page. The two versions are not completely identical in wording; the quotations are tied in skillfully in Dutch.

3. Harm Wansink, *Politieke Wetenschappen aan de Leidse Universiteit,* pp. 5–17.

4. Joseph Lecler, *Geschichte der Religionsfreiheit,* II, seventh part, chapter 6; see also Heppe, *Dogmatik,* pp. 525–34. On 5 October 1611, fifty-six copies of Vorstius's *De Deo* were burned in England. See note 5, below.

5. C. v.d. Woude, *Sibrandus Lubbertus* (Kampen, 1963), pp. 198–308.

6. Ecclesiastically, the provincial states were the "magistrates" to call a synod.

7. *Synodus tot Dordrecht* (Dort: I. J. Canin, 1619), 96 pp.

8. Virgil, *Aeneid,* Book V, vv. 362–484. Grotius had brought up the possibility for such a comparison to the Trojan Dares, the eventual loser himself, by accusing Lubbertus on p. 48 (Latin version) of having changed his Trojan helmet for a Greek one after defeat, as in *Aeneid,* Book II, v. 389.

9. Noted by v.d. Woude, *Lubbertus,* p. 267.

10. Virgil, *Aeneid.* Latin-German Heimeran ed. by J. Götte, p. 721. On dutifulness see Th. Ulrich, *Pietas (pius) als politischer Begiff im römischen Staate,* Historische Untersuchungen Heft 6 (Breslau, 1930), pp. 28–33.

11. See Chapter 2, note 30. The term *pietas* also has a separate origin and goes back to the Roman lawyer Papinian, *Digesta* 28, 7, 15. See also Cicero, *De Natura Deorum* 1:116, in which he defines *pietas* as "justice versus the gods."

12. *Lubbertus,* p. 286 ff.

13. Literally, the permission to lecture. For theologians it was based on the right to preach.

14. The majority of reformed theologians, Lubbertus, Richard Hooker, as well as Grotius in his mature years, adhered to the so-called "infralapsaristic" point of view, which sees man's fall from paradise as an expression of Adam and Eve's lack of perseverance in obeying God's command. They were not created in order to sin; rather they were created not to sin, and took the forbidden, hence wrong, choice. The supralapsarian (f.i. Th. Beza, Calvin's successor in Geneva) believes that the occurrence of the corruption was predestined by God before the fall. The *confessio Belgica,* 16, adopts the infralapsarian point of view. Cf. Heppe, *Dogmatik,* pp. 118–19, 127. Cf. also Chapter 2, note 30.

15. Wansink, *Politieke,* pp. 106–40.

16. In Lubbertus's refutation, *Responsio ad Pietatem Hugonis Grotii.*

17. As is proven by the drafting of provincial militia by Grotius, in order to protect ecclesiastic law and order in Holland.

18. Richard Hooker, *Of the Laws of Ecclesiastical Polity* (1593–97), with which Grotius was vaguely familiar, according to his letter to Casaubonus of 19 December 1613, *BW* I 289.

19. As it considered herself catholic with a small c; see Heppe, *Dogmatik*, p. 245 ff. The term *ius circa sacra* was coined by J. Lipsius in his main work, *Politica*.

20. T. H. L. Parker, *John Calvin: A Biography* (Philadelphia: Westminster, 1975), p. 15.

21. *BW* I no. 310, 19. 1. 1613, 289.

22. Karl Barth, *Kirchliche Dogmatik,* vol. I/2 (Zollikon, 1960), p. 617, note 8.

23. Based with modifications on Calvin's famous *Institutio(nes) Christianae Religionis;* see François Wendel, *Calvin: The Origins and Development of His Religious Thought* (London: Collins, 1963; tr. from the French original, 1950), pp. 212–14.

24. *Ecclesiastical Polity,* vol. 1, Book IV, pp. 412–21.

25. Schlüter, *Die Theologie des Hugo Grotius,* p. 73, corrected by Bohatec, *ZRG*. Kanonistische *Abteilung* 35 (1948):64–106.

26. *Godts-Diensticheyt* (1613), TMD 823, p. 7 ff.

27. See Chapter 2.

28. See Chapter 2.

29. Second chapter, "Verwerphinge," 4:31.

30. TMD 922 note 1.

31. Schlüter, as in note 25, p. 47.

32. Heppe, *Dogmatik,* locus XVIII, p. 378. See Gustaf Aulén, *Christus Victor* (London: S.P.C.K., 1931; rpt. 1978).

33. "Clemency" is used here in the Erasmian and ultimately pagan Senecaesque meaning; see A. M. Hugo, *Calvijn en Seneca: . . . Calvijns Commentaar op Seneca, De Clementia, anno 1532* (Groningen/Djakarta: Wolters, 1957).

34. *Defensio fidei,* p. 14 (= *Opera Omnia Theologica,* 3:306).

35. Neither Grotius's contemporaries nor modern dogmaticists side with him on this issue; see Heppe, *Dogmatik,* p. 378. The controversy goes back to the Italian brothers Sozzini, antitrinitarians both.

36. Grotius's *Apologeticus* will only be considered briefly in Chapter 6.

37. The formula implies that a Christian believer becomes saved by faith alone, rather than by faith and good deeds together.

38. Haentjens, *Hugo de Groot,* p. 135, and note *recte* 179 (misprinted 107).

39. Konrad Repgen, "Grotius Papizans," in *Reformata Reformanda. Festgabe für Hubert Jedin,* ed. E. Iserloh and K. Repgen (Münster: Aschendorff, 1965), pp. 370–400.

40. This traditional title was not coined by Justinian, but was attached to the Corpus later in the Middle Ages.

41. Subsequently attached to this code were the so-called *Novellae Constitutiones*. These were emended statutes promulgated during the rule of Justinian, A.D. 535–65, and by emperors following him: cf. P. Jörs-W. Kunkel-L. Wenger, *Römisches Privatrecht*, 3rd ed. (Berlin/Göttingen/Heidelberg, 1949), p. 45; see also R. Sohm, L. Mitteis, and L. Wenger, *Institutionen. Geschichte und System des römischen Privatrechts*, 17th ed. (München & Leipzig, 1928). We omit the Novellae from further discussion since Grotius devotes to them only 7 pp. of 415; *Florum Sparsio*, TMD 791.

42. These *Institutes* served as a model for Grotius's *Introduction to Holland's Jurisprudence;* see discussion at the close of this chapter.

43. *Digesta* in Latin, πανδέκται in Greek, meaning "case decision." A reasonably good introduction by H. F. Jolowicz, *Historical Introduction to the Study of Roman Law* (Cambridge: Cambridge University Press, 1952), Chapter 28.

44. Fr. Wieacker, *Privatrechtsgeschichte der Neuzeit*, 2d ed. (Göttingen: 1967), p. 289.

45. See p. 36.

46. Our TMD 795 edition lists several indexes on pp. 333–78.

47. Quoted in part in TMD 795 5.

48. Quoting from Aristotle, Philemon, Stobaeus, Chrysippos, Cicero, Gellius, Ulpian, and others.

49. Dumbauld, *The Life*, p. 170; Grotius quotes from further Greek and Latin writers.

50. In Justinian's *Corpus Juris Civilis*, ed. in 3 volumes by P. Krüger *(Institutiones/Codex);* Th. Mommsen, *Digesta;* R. Schoell/G. Kroll, *Novellae* (Berlin: Weidmann, 1928/29; last rpt. 1954/59); some of Grotius's emendations, mostly found in the *Digests*, are accepted; cf. Dumbauld, *The Life*, p. 170.

51. Dumbauld, *The Life*, p. 177. We find Grotius's comments on commercial law, and particularly on monopolies of relevance, in *Florum Sparsio*, TMD 795 287.

52. *Grotiana* 9 (1941/42):61 ff.

53. *De Jure Praedae Commentarius*, treated below.

54. TMD 541 note 8; H. Grotius, *The Freedom of the Seas* (New York: Arno Press, 1972); Jonathan Ziskind, "International Law and Ancient Sources: Grotius and Selden," *Review of Politics* 35 (Notre Dame, 1973):537–59, makes the point that Grotius's style is "lucid and Ciceronian."

55. Whether as public counsellor or defense lawyer in the case itself has remained controversial so far.

56. TMD 541 note 11, as the sixth title by Grotius and of several others to follow, including even his *Poemata Collecta;* see F. H. Reusch, *Der Index*

der verbotenen Bücher (1885), pp. 102–6; TMD, *Bibliographie des Ecrits sur H. Grotius* (1961), 184–92, and Chapter 6.

57. Fahl, *Der Grundsatz der Freiheit der Meere,* p. 49 ff., on France; p. 90 ff. on Britain; p. 116 ff. on the Netherlands (Köln, 1969).

58. The source of this law is Augustus's appropriation law *(lex Julia Peculatus)* embraced by the *Digests* 48:13:1, and the *Codex* 9:28.

59. This circular argument was by no means an invention by Grotius, but was already Roman law; the principle was called *mare—res communis omnium,* implying everybody's fishing right everywhere on the high seas; it is laid down in *Digests* 1:8:2:1 and *Institutes* 2:1:1.   60. Founded and privileged by Queen Elizabeth I on 31 December 1600, a privilege renewed by James I on 31 May 1609 immediately after the Spanish-Dutch Truce.

61. Fahl, *Grundsatz,* p. 110 ff., based on the results of van Eysinga in *Bibliotheca Visseriana* 15 (1940) and G. N. Clark in *Bibliotheca Visseriana* 17 (1951).

62. I, 3 § XXI, 2, 4–5: *debellatio* and its influence on sovereignty; on export monopolies see *DJBP* II, 2 § XXIV, which Grotius thought justifiable on the basis of fair price for luxuries, but not for necessities of life.

63. This is the principal result of Fr. de Pauw's study *Grotius and the Law of the Sea* (1965), pp. 73–75. For related problems see also J. K. Oudendijk, *Status and Extent of Adjacent Waters* (Leiden, 1970), 160 pp.

64. Joannes Selden, *Mare Clausum seu de Dominio Maris libri duo* (London: Meighen, 1635). Selden's style is labeled by Ziskind (see note 54) as "thick, turgid and defying translation" (559) but "methodologically sound."

65. De Pauw, *Grotius,* p. 64.

66. *Mare Liberum,* Chapter 1: *"Deus hoc ipse per naturam loquitur, ..."*

67. *Georgica* II, 109; *Aeneid* VI, 847 ff., esp. 853.

68. *Elegies,* IV, 47 ff. Unnoticed so far, it is taken over by Grotius from his *De Jure Praedae Commentarius,* Chapter 15, *Classics of International Law Edition* (1950), p. 335. In the commentary it is preceded by "press on, press on, o nation of seafarers!"

69. "In arrangement and logical order, in cogency of argument and in citation of authorities, this work has few equals"; Dumbauld, *The Life,* p. 29.

70. This distinction becomes clear, if one recognizes "private" as abstractly standing for the VOC, and "public" for the Staten Generaal. The book ends with a prayer to God that the enemies of Holland be overthrown, the implication being that traders of true religion and legally valid contracts make retainable booty in just wars.

71. Causes for justification are listed as self-defense; protection and recovery of property; other belongings; and punishment of injuries.

72. See beginning of this chapter.

73. The idea of reimbursement for losses seems to head in the direction of lucrative maritime insurance business.

74. "Revenue from prizes supports the public treasuries" (p. 339); "at the saving of the taxpayer's purse" (340); "and for the benefit of Dutch commercial enterprise" (343).

75. Dumbauld, *The Life*, exaggerates by calling them "controlling principles of legal philosophy" (p. 30).

76. Grotius plays on *jus, Jovis, jubere,* and *jussum* in the original text. See *"a quo Jovis nomine ius Latinis dictum probaliter dici potest," DJBP* Prolegomena 12.

77. In the Latin ms., found in 1864 and edited in 1868 by H. G. Hamaker (TMD 684), the "rules" (= *regulae*) and the "norms" (= *leges*) are intertwined. Dumbauld, *The Life,* pp. 32–37, shows where these rules and norms recur in DJBP.

78. Norm XIII, Dumbauld, *The Life,* p. 37; under "divine volitional law" Grotius heads the "law of nature" and the "law of nations."

79. See S. van Oorde, *Het 3rde Hoofdstuk . . . etc. Redux Serie Number 9* (Zwolle: Tjeenk Willink, 1962), p. 67.

80. G. A. Finch in: Preface to TMD 687, I, p. XIX.

81. *De Jure Praedae,* Chapter 15, final phrase.

82. Van Eysinga, *Huigh de Groot,* p. 24; Dumbauld, *The Life,* p. 41.

83. See Th. Viehweg, "Historische Perspektiven der juristischen Argumentation," in *Archiv für Rechts- und Sozialphilosophie. Beiheft. Neue Folge 7* (Wiesbaden: Steiner, 1972), pp. 62–73, esp. p. 65 f.

84. Italics are ours. Quoted from the translation of John D. Maguire, *The Classics of International Law,* ed. J. B. Scott; vol. 2 ed. F. W. Kelsey (Oxford, 1925); rpt. in *American Journal of International Law* 35 (1941):205 ff.

85. See W. Fikentscher, *Methoden des Rechts,* 4:697.

86. *Fide et Perfidia,* p. 149.

87. Of the twenty Genesis quotations in "Prize" only two reappear exactly in DJBP. Grotius quotes fewer sources and authors in "Prize," but uses them more often than in "War."

88. Carl v. Clausewitz's famous dictum on "war being but a continuation of politics with different means" (*Vom Kriege,* 1832) is watered-down Grotian.

89. R. Wilenius, "The Social and Political Theory of F. Suárez," *Acta Philosophica Fennica* 15 (Helsinki, 1963); the influence of Justus Lipsius's

Politicorum sive civilis doctrinae libri sex (1589 ff.), books 5 and 6, on *DJBP*, has not yet been determined.

90. As well as—according to *DJBP* II, 15, 8—supraconfessional, rather than, as we would say today, international and ecumenical; see Fr. Wieacker, *Privatrechtsgeschichte,* pp. 287–301, esp. p. 289.

91. Quotation found in Fikentscher, 5:681, from *Liber proverbiorum* III, cap. LIII.

92. See H. Welzel, *Naturrecht,* pp. 123–29.

93. *DJBP* I, 1, 11, 2 and I, 1, 10, 1.

94. In *Inleidinghe*—see this chapter—he translates *lex naturalis* as "inborn law," leading ultimately to a "bill of rights"; I, cap. 1, 2, 5.

95. This edition is preceded by sixteen Latin ones.

96. Jean Barbeyrac, *Le Droit de la Guerre et de la Paix par Hugues Grotius.* Nouvelle Traduction (Basle, 1746), vols. I/II; 1:x; a very helpful edition.

97. *BW* II no. 841 to the librarian Pierre du Puy, p. 298.

98. Van Eysinga, *Huigh de Groot,* p. 94.

99. J. Huizinga, *Tien Studiën* (Haarlem, 1926), p. 122.

100. Van Eysinga, *Huigh de Groot,* p. 97.

101. Heinz Meyer, *Die Zahlenallegorese im Mittelalter. Münstersche Mittelalterschriften* 25 (München, 1975), pp. 128, 164.

102. V. F. Hopper, *Medieval Number Symbolism* (New York, 1938), pp. 36, 43, 102, 124.

103. W. Kirfel, "Zahlen- und Farbensymbole," *Saeculum* 12 (1961):237–47, esp. 239; so also from the specific view point of the number symbolism in the law, B. E. Siebs, *Weltbild, symbolische Zahl und Verfassung* (Aalen: Scientia, 1969), pp. 86–89.

104. Meyer, *Zahlenallegorese,* p. 129.

105. "The use of fifteen was more habitual then than now by virtue of . . . scientific usage"; Hopper, *Medieval,* p. 127.

106. That he studied "Pythagorean theology" young Grotius states in *Dichtwerken* (= *Sacra*) I 1A in 1601, p. 294.

107. *Gids for de Groot De Jure Belli ac Pacis* (Leiden: Brill, 1945), p. 13.

108. J. Huizinga, *Nederlandse Beschaving in de Zeventiende Eeuw,* 4th ed. (1972), pp. 162 f., 164 f.

109. Stated authoritatively by R. Feenstra in *Fata Iuris Romana* (Leiden, 1974), pp. 338–63. This is not to denigrate the immense efforts devoted to *DJBP* by Ph. Molhuysen in his eminently practical edition of 1919, which we used, or the formal elegance achieved by Dr. B. J. A. De Kanter van Hettinga Tromp in her Leiden edition of 1939, the best in the whole field.

110. Wieacker, *Privatrechtsgeschichte,* p. 290.

111. There is agreement on this among Knight, Molhuysen, Eysinga, and Wellschmied, *TRG* 20 (1952), p. 425.

112. Several complaints voiced from *BW* II no. 594 (to his wife) to *BW* IV no. 1525. That lack of books at Loevestein explains the fortunate failure of quoting other authors, see Wellschmied, *TRG*, p. 430.

113. See Chapter 2.

114. Petrus Ramus (= Pierre de la Ramée), born 1515, murdered in the Bartholomew's Night Massacre, 1572, liked to express high thoughts in rigidly bifurcating charts. In respect to this method of dichotomization, Grotius was influenced by J. Arminius; cf. C. Bangs, *Arminius* (1958), p. 58 f. See also the five-step system chart representing the "law of nature" to his brother Willem, then a student of law at Leiden, in *BW* I no. 405, p. 391. See also W. J. Ong, *Ramus* (Cambridge: Cambridge University Press, 1958), p. 202.

115. The corresponding sources in the *Institutes* are put together by Wellschmied in *TRG* p. 390 ff.

116. The dichotomization of the fourth table is the most significant one, as it puts one part, possession, under good versus bad faith.

117. The attempts by Prof. R. Feenstra to claim Grotius's *De Aequitate* (TMD 810) as omitted prolegomena to *Inleidinghe*, first in *TRG* 35 (1967):444–84, then in collaboration with J. E. Scholtens in *TRG* 42 (1974):201–42, are unconvincing. To our knowledge there is not a single instance known that Grotius treats in his prolegomena matters different from those of the main body itself. Here, we believe, the void left by the lacking prolegomenon—for the revised letter is an exordium only—is filled by the tables. The whole area of *aequus* (*Digests* 1:1:1), which Grotius purposefully leaves out in *Inl.* I:i, could be considered a prime witness to Fikentscher's theory of a *"Fallnorm"* (*Methoden des Rechts*, vol. 5), and keeps an intellectual proximity, if any, to DJBP II, 16, 26. *De Interpretatione.* Thus *De Aequitate* is related more to equiprudence, not as much to jurisprudence, narrowly speaking. See also point 8b of *State Authority over Church Governance*.

118. Meyer, *Zahlenallegorese*, p. 177, note 101.

119. Paul Merula, *Synopsis Praxeos Civilis: Maniere van Procederen*. First edition dates from 1592.

120. Wellschmied, *TRG*, pp. 391–95.

121. *Hugonis Grotii Institutiones juris hollandici e belgico in latinum sermonem translatae a Joanne van der Linde, J.V.D.* (who died in 1855), ed. Herman Fr. W. D. Fischer with a preface in English. *Rechtshistorisch Instituut. Leiden.* serie I, 3 (Haarlem, 1962). The leading Dutch edition is by F. Dovring, H. F. W. D. Fischer, and E. M. Meijers, Universitaire Pers Leiden, 1952.

122. *Grotius' Invloed op de Nederlandse Rechtsterminologie.* Diss., Liège, 1968–69 in 2 vols. of 572 pp; see p. 552 ff. The remaining 153 legal terms Grotius took from medieval Dutch. We did not check their exact survival percentage.

123. Grotius created sixty-eight legal terms alone according to Esch-Pelgroms.

124. Dumbauld, *The Life,* p. 131 summarizing *Inl.* I:2:2.

125. *BW* IV no. 1711, p. 474, in a letter to his brother-in-law.

Chapter Six

1. G. Oestreich, *Seventeenth Century Leiden University* (1975), p. 185; 4,300 letters from and to Lipsius are reported by Oestreich to have been preserved; Justus Lipsius, *Institutio Epistolica Opera Omnia,* 2d ed. (Amsterdam, 1591; Moretus, 1600); A. Gerlo and H. Vervliet, *Inventaire de la Correspondance de J. Lipse* (1967).

2. The data were kindly supplied from the files of Dra. Paula Witkam, the present editor of *Briefwisseling,* as of vol. 11 (1640), Dec. '81.

3. Only one-fourth of his correspondence is written before 1633, his fiftieth year. By number, the halfway mark is reached during the year 1639. From then to 1645 he writes/receives 50 percent of his preserved correspondence. Thus Grotius cannot be compared to Lipsius as an elegant letter writer.

4. H. C. Rogge, *Brieven van en aan M. v. Reigersbergh* (Leiden: Brill, 1902); Robert Fruin, *Allerliefste van Hugo de Groot* (rpt. The Hague: B. Bakker, 1957).

5. So noted by van Eysinga, *Huigh de Groot,* p. 7.

6. Official letters omitting the address "Excellency" were left unanswered; H. Wehberg, *Hugo Grotius* (1956), p. 52.

7. According to A. Eijffinger, "Het Handschrift Papenbroeck 10," *LIAS* 7:1 (1980):96 ff., Jan de Groot dealt with exporting Delft beer to Dantzig.

8. Fockema Andreae, *De Nederlandse Staat onder de Republiek* (Amsterdam: Noord Holland, 1975), p. 16.

9. Dumbauld, *The Life,* p. 88, note 22. The structure falls into four parts: the justification of the States of Holland's course of action in the alleged religious controversies; the procedural defects of this High Court's condemnation of the accused; a rebuttal of every phrase of his sentence; and finally a vicarious defense of Grotius's coaccused. These four apologetic masses are distributed unevenly as follows: (1) 45 percent; (2) 13 percent; (3a) 38 percent; (3b) 4 percent.

Notes and References

10. See Den Tex, *Oldenbarnevelt*, 3:704 ff., who distinguishes legality from justification, although seventeenth-century juridical dictionaries, according to Esch-Pelgroms, 2:531, do not list such derivative of *wet*. That the *crimen laesae majestatis* could be committed against the Counts of Holland was first established in the fourteenth century by Philips van Leiden, *De Cura rei publicae et sorte principantis,* ed. R. Fruin and P. C. Molhuysen (The Hague, 1900), 49:46–48.

11. Still adhered to by Hendrik Gerlach, *Het Proces tegen Oldenbarnevelt en de Maximen in den Staet*, Diss., Leiden (Haarlem: Tjeenk Willink, 1965).

12. Den Tex, *Oldenbarnevelt*, 3:771.

13. *Sophompaneas*, v. 1229–30, *coelestis calor*.

14. See Christian Gellinek: "Hugo Grotius und Gerard Ter Borch: Neues zum Kampf um den Westfälischen Frieden," *Simpliciana* 3 (1982).

15. See Epistle Dedicatory to Vossius in his foreword to Sophompaneas: "The common study of all Literature is a very strong bond."

16. Van Vollenhoven, "Grotius and Geneva," in *Bibliotheca Visseriana* (Leiden: Brill, 1926), Grotius' Influence, 3:34–44.

17. Ter Meulen and Diermanse, *Bibliographie des Ecrits sur Hugo Grotius* (1961).

18. Horace Bushnell, *The Vicarious Sacrifice* (New York: C. Scribner & Co., 1866).

19. He even called Pufendorf his "chief guide and spokesman." See Scholar's Facsimile Edition (Gainesville, Fla., 1958, based on the Boston editions of 1717 and 1772).

20. "Ein Kapitel aus der Geschichte der amerikanischen Erklärung der Menschenrechte, John Wise und Samuel Pufendorf," in *Rechtsprobleme in Staat und Kirche. Festschrift für Rudolf Smend zum 70. Geburtstag*. Göttinger Rechtswissenschaftliche Studien (1952), 3:387–411.

21. *The Classics of International Law,* ed. J. B. Scott, S. Pufendorf, *De Jure Naturae et Gentium* (Oxford, 1934), Introduction by Walter Simons, pp. 13a–66a.

22. We quote from Welzel, "John Wise," namely the edition of 1860 by I. S. Clark.

23. Van Vollenhoven, "Grotius and Geneva," p. 35.

24. Roscoe Pound, "Grotius and the Science of Law," *American Journal of International Law* 19 (1925):685–88, esp. 687.

25. See Adda B. Bozeman, in *Grotiana* 1 (1980):65–124.

26. A first attempt is made by Christian Gellinek, "Literatur und Politik bei Grotius, Opitz und Milton: Ein Vergleich Christlich-Politischer Grundgedanken," in *Daphnis Sonderheft Martin Opitz,* ed. B. Becker-Cantarino (Berlin, 1982).

27. W. A. P. Smit, *Van Pascha tot Noah: Een Verkenning van Vondel's Drama's naar Continuiteit en Ontwikkeling in hun Grondmotief en Structuur*, 3 vols. in: *Zwolse Reeks van Taal- en Letterkundige Studies*, Nr.s 5A-C (Zwolle: Tjeenk Willink, 1956, 1959, 1962).

28. K. Langvik Johannessen, *Zwischen Himmel und Erde: Eine Studie über Joost van den Vondels biblische Tragödie in gattungsgeschichtlicher Perspektive. Germanistische Schriftenreihe der norwegischen Universitäten und Hochschulen Nr. 1* (Oslo, 1963), p. 91.

29. Christian Gellinek, "Wettlauf um die Wahrheit der Christlichen Religion," in *Simpliciana* (Bern: Francke, 1980), 2:71–90; "Hugo de Groots und Martin Opitzens Glaubensverteidigungen von 1622 und 1631," in *Akten des VI. Internationalen Germanisten-Kongresses* (Basel, 1980), 4:33–39; Malte Diesselhorst, *Die Lehre des Hugo Grotius vom Versprechen. Forschungen zur neueren Privatrechtsgeschichte*, vol. 6 (Köln/Graz: Böhlau, 1959). For reservations see J. C. van Oven, *Tijdschrift voor Rechtsgeschiedenis* 29 (1961):328–81.

30. Reinhardt Brandt, *Eigentumstheorien von Grotius bis Kant*. Problemata Frommann-Holzboog 31 (Stuttgart, 1974), pp. 31–49, a superficial treatment; much more thoroughgoing is Robert Feenstra, "Der Eigentumsbegriff bei Hugo Grotius in Licht einiger mittelalterlicher und spätscholastischer Quellen," in *Festschrift für Franz Wieacker zum 70. Geburtstag* (Göttingen, 1978), pp. 209–34. See also *DJBP* II, 10:2:1.

31. Giambattista Vico, *Opere*, vol. 1. *De Uno universi iuris principio et fine uno. Proloquium*, 20: "Jurisconsultus generis humani."

Selected Bibliography

PRIMARY SOURCES

The original seventeenth-century edition as indicated hereunder by the appropriate Ter Meulen-Diermanse (TMD) number is used for discussions and quotations unless otherwise indicated, since no critical Opera Omnia Edition of Hugo Grotius exists so far. Round-bracketed figures indicate number of editions which appeared during the author's lifetime (until 1645). Textbook editions are given in Roman capitals.

Curr. No.	Editions	Title (written)	Place	Year	Trans. Lang.	TMD No.
1.	2 (1)	MARTIANI CAPELLAE SATYRICON 8^0 336 pp.	Leiden	1599	—	411
2.	10 (2)	SYNTAGMA ARATEORUM 4^0 128 pp.	Leiden	1600	—	413
3.	6 (1)	Adamus Exul Tragoedia 4^0 55 pp.	The Hague	1601	2	21
4.	22 (7)	Christus Patiens Tragoedia 8^0 61 pp.	Leiden	1608	3	31
5.						
a.	24 (13)	Mare Liberum (Ch. 12 of 5b) 8^0 42 pp. (1st ed. anonymous)	Leiden	1609	5	541
b.	4 (0)	De Jure Praedae (1604/06) 8^0 359 pp.	The Hague	1868	2	684
6.	20 (11)	De Antiquitate Reipublicae Batavicae 4^0 60 pp.	Leiden	1610	3	691

147

Curr. No.	Editions	Title (written)	Place	Year	Trans. Lang.	TMD No.
7.	9 (0)	Annales [1559–88] & Historiae [1588–1609] De Rebus Belgicis 4⁰ 559 pp.	Amsterdam	1657	3	741
8.						
a.	8 (6)	Ordinum Hollandiae ac Westfrisiae Pietas 4⁰ 126 pp.	Leiden	1613	2	817
b.	11 (0)	De Imperio Summarum Potestatum Circa Sacra 8⁰ 391 pp. (written by 1614)	Paris	1647	2	894
9.	34 (9)	LUCANI PHARSALIA 8⁰ 432 pp.	Leiden	1614	—	423
10.	7 (5)	Poemata Collecta (edited by his brother Willem) 8⁰ 548 pp.	Leiden	1616	—	1
11.	15 (4)	Defensio fidei catholicae de Satisfactione Christi adversus Faustum Socinum Senensem 4⁰ 199 pp. (started 1614)	Leiden	1617	3	922
12.	45 (13)	T'Samensprake over den Doop 4⁰ 13 pp. (1618)	sine loco	1618	5	59
13.						
a.	12 (4)	Bewys van de waere Godsdienst 4⁰ 111 pp. (1619–21)	sine loco	1622	2	143
b.	147 (15)	De Veritate Religionis Christianae 12⁰ 202 pp. (started 1623)	Leiden	1627	11	944
14.	10 (2)	DICTA POETARUM quae apud Ioann. STOBAEUM 4⁰	Paris	1623	—	458

Selected Bibliography 149

Curr. No.	Editions	Title (written)	Place	Year	Trans. Lang.	TMD No.
		564 pp. Den Haag-Loevestein (started 1618; arranged by subject)				
15.	115 (12)	De Jure Belli ac Pacis 4⁰ 786 pp. (started 1622 near Paris)	Paris	1625	9	565
16.	1 (1)	EXCERPTA EX TRAGOEDIIS & COMOEDIIS GRAECIS 4⁰ 1006 pp. (started 1606; arranged by authors)	Paris	1626	—	468
17.	7 (2)	EURIPIDIS TRAGOEDIA PHOENISSAE 8⁰ 125 pp.	Paris	1630	1	496
18.	35 (9)	Inleidinghe tot de Hollandsche Rechtsgeleerdheid 4⁰ 186 pp. at Loevestein (1619–21)	The Hague	1631	2	757
19.	41 (7)	Sophompaneas Tragoedia 4⁰ 169 pp.	Amsterdam	1635	2	157
20.	8 (2)	C. CORNELIUS TACITUS EX I. LIPSII EDITIONE 12⁰ 746 pp.	Leiden	1640	—	515
21.	22 (1)	Annotationes in Novum Testamentum 6⁰ 1060 pp.	Amsterdam	1641 ff.	2	1135
22.	10 (1)	Annotata ad Vetum Testamentum 4⁰ 1717 pp.	Amsterdam	1644 ff.	—	1137
23.	5 (3)	Florum Sparsio ad Ius Iustinianaeum 4⁰ 415 pp.	Paris	1642	—	791

Curr. No.	Editions	Title (written)	Place	Year	Trans. Lang.	TMD No.
24.	12 (4)	Votum pro Pace Ecclesiastica 8⁰ 166 pp.	Paris?	1642	2	1183
25.	6 (1)	Historia Gotthorum, Vandalorum & Langobardorum 8⁰ 1178 pp.	Amsterdam	1655	1	735

Other posthumous editions not meant by Grotius for publication in this form:

(26.)	6 (0)	Philosophorum sententiae de fato 4⁰ 384 pp.	Paris	1648	—	523
(27.)	2 (0)	Anthologia Graeca cum versione latina 4⁰ CLVI + 2732 pp. in 4 vols. (started 1603)	Utrecht	1795 ff.	—	534
(28.)	1 (0)	Parallelon rerumpublicarum 8⁰ lii + 312 pp. in 3 vols. (started ca. 1600)	Haarlem	1801 ff.	—	750
28.	659	(136) Editions (textbooks printed in CAPITAL letters)		1599–1980	0–11	

SECONDARY SOURCES

1. Bibliographies

Ter Meulen, Jacob et Diermanse, P. J. J. *Bibliographie des écrits imprimés de Hugo Grotius*. The Hague: Martinus Nijhoff, 1950. 8⁰ 708 pp.; containing over 1,200 entries. A masterful annotated bibliography, the

Selected Bibliography 151

basis on which all further Grotius research has to rest. My debt is here gratefully acknowledged.

———. *Bibliographie des écrits sur Hugo Grotius imprimés au XVIIe siècle.* The Hague: Martinus Nijhoff, 1961. 8⁰. 224 pp.

2. General and Seventeenth-Century Reading List

Berger, Adolf. *Encyclopedic Dictionary of Roman Law.* Transactions of the American Philosophical Society. Philadelphia, 1953. 474 pp.

Meijer, Reinder P. *Literature of the Low Countries: A Short History of Dutch Literature in the Netherlands and Belgium.* 2d ed. The Hague Boston: Martinus Nijhoff, 1978. 402 pp.

Molhuysen, P. C., en Blok, P. J. *Nieuw Nederlandsch Biographisch Woordenboek.* Leiden: Sijthoff, 1911–1937.

3. Interpretations of Hugo Grotius's Life and Works

Shorter Introductions

Fruin, Robert. "Hugo de Groot en Maria van Reigersbergh." In: *De Gids,* 2. Amsterdam, 1858. Reprinted in *Allerliefste van Hugo de Groot.* Ooievaar 58. The Hague: Bakker/Daamen, 1957, pp. 9–103.

Huizinga, Johan. "Hugo de Groot en zijn Eeuw." *De Gids* 89, no. 10 (1925):1–16.

———. "Grotius' Plaats in de Geschiedenis van den menschelijken Geest." Rede te Gent 25 December 1925. Reprinted in *Tien Studiën.* Haarlem: Tjeenk Willink, 1926, pp. 117–25.

Lee, R. W. *Hugo Grotius.* Annual Lecture on a Mastermind. British Academy, 16. London, 1930. 60 pp.

Esch-Pelgroms, M. "Levensgeschiedenis van Hugo de Groot." I/II. *Revue des Langues Vivantes. Tijdschrift voor Levende Talen* 36 (1971):42 pp., being an excerpt from "Grotius' Invloed op de Nederlandse Rechtsterminologie." Ph.D. diss., University of Liège, Belgium, 1968/69. 572 pp.

Monographs
Eighteenth Century

Brandt, Caspar, and Cattenburgh, Adriaan van. *Historie van het leven des heeren Huig de Groot.* Dordrecht/Amsterdam: Van Braan en Onder de Linden, 1727; 2d ed., 1732.

Burigny, Jean L. De. *Vie de Grotius avec l'Histoire de ses ouvrages et les negociations auxquelles il fut employe.* I/II. Paris: Debure, 1752; Amsterdam: Marc Michel Dey, 1754. Translated into English, 1754; German, 1755. 596 pp.

Nineteenth Century
Butler, Charles. *The Life of Hugo Grotius with Brief Minutes of the Civil, Ecclesiastical and Literary History of the Netherlands.* London: Murray, 1826. 259 pp.
Luden, Heinrich. *Hugo Grotius nach seinen Schicksalen und Schriften dargestellt.* Berlin: J. F. Unger, 1806. 342 pp. Translated into Dutch, 1830.
Vries, Jeronimo de. *Hugo de Groot en Maria van Reigersbergen.* Amsterdam: Ten Brink, 1827.

Twentieth Century
Dumbauld, Edward. *The Life and Legal Writings of Hugo Grotius.* Norman: University of Oklahoma Press, 1969. 206 pp. A valuable essay collection.
Eysinga, Willem J. M. van. *Huigh de Groot: Een Schets.* Haarlem: Tjeenk Willink, 1945. 141 pp.
Hallema, A. *Hugo de Groot: Het Delftsch Orakel 1583–1645: Een Levenschets van een groot Nederlander uit de 17e Eeuw.* The Hague: Stols, 1942. 255 pp. Patriotically inspiring.
Knight, William Stanley MacBean. *The Life and Works of Hugo Grotius.* The Grotius Society Publications, No. 4. London, 1925. 304 pp. Reprinted New York: Oceana Publications, 1962; The British Institute of International or Comparative Law. London: Wildy, 1962.
Vreeland, Hamilton, Jr. *Hugo Grotius: The Father of the Modern Science of International Law.* New York: Oxford University Press, 1917. 258 pp. Heavily dependent on Brandt and Cattenburgh.

Iconography
Beresteyn, Eltjo A. Van. *Iconographie van Hugo Grotius met 65 portretten.* The Hague: Martinus Nijhoff, 1929. 135 pp.

Lawsuit of 1618/19
Fruin, Robert J. *Verhooren en andere bescheiden betreffende het rechtsgeding van Hugo de Groot.* Utrecht: Kenink & Zoon, 1871.

4. Studies on Hugo Grotius as Poet
Vollenhoven, Cornelis van. "De Groots Sophompaneas." In: *Mnemosyne.* Nova Series 51. Leiden: Brill, 1923, pp. 342–64.
Bodkins, E. H. "The Minor Poetry of Hugo Grotius." *Transactions of the Grotius Society founded 1915.* 13. London, 1928, pp. 95–128.
Ellinger, Georg. *Geschichte der neulateinischen Lyrik in den Niederlanden.* 3:1. Abteilung der Geschichte der neulateinischen Literatur Deutschlands. Berlin: de Gruyter, 1933, pp. 344; 201–24.

Kluge, Otto. *Die Dichtung des Hugo Grotius im Rahmen der neulateinischen Kunstpoesie. Mnemosyne Bibliothecae Classicae Batavicae.* Leiden: Brill: vol. 6 (1938), pp. 1–82; 8 (1940), 199–234, 257–82 = 144 pp.

Eijffinger, Arthur C. "Ter Inleiding." In: *De Dichtwerken van Hugo de Groot.* Tweede Deel, Pars A en B. Edited by B. L. Meulenbroek. Assen: Van Gorcum, 1978, pp. 9–36.

———. "De Dichter Hugo de Groot." In *Forum der Letteren: Tijdschrift voor Taal- en Letterkunde.* Muiderberg: Coutinho, September 1978, pp. 212–26.

———. "Prent en Puntdicht: Grotius' Maurits-Epigrammen." *Oud Holland.* 92:3 (1978):161–206.

———. Inventaris van de latijnse poëzie van Hugo Grotius. Unpublished Folder. The Hague, 1980. 137 pp.

———. *Grotius Poeta: Aspecten van Hugo Grotius' Dichterschap.* Amsterdam dissertation defended 30 June 1981. The Hague: n.p., 1981. 344 pp.; is essentially the material contained in the other four publications/inventarization cited herewith, with a new summary on the *Poemata Collecta.*

5. Research on Hugo Grotius's Main Scientific Areas

Theology

Schlüter, Joachim. *Die Theologie des Hugo Grotius.* Göttingen: Vandenhoeck & Ruprecht, 1919. 120 pp.

Unnik, W. C. van. "Hugo de Groot als uitlegger van het Nieuwe Testament." *Nederlandsch archief voor kerkgeschiedenis,* Nieuwe Serien Deel 2t T1o32):12I48.

Haentjens, Anton H. *Hugo de Groot als Godsdienstig Denker.* Amsterdam: Ploegsma, 1946. 176 pp.

Voeltzel, René. "La methode theologique de Hugo Grotius." *Revue d'Histoire et de Philosophie Religieuse: Etudes Critiques,* 1952, pp. 126–33.

Woude, C. van der. *Hugo Grotius en zijn "Pietas Ordinum Hollandiae ac Westfrisiae vindicata."* Rede. Kampen: Kok, 1961, pp. 1–41.

Wolf, Dieter. *Die Irenik des Hugo Grotius nach ihren Prinzipien und biographisch-geistesgeschichtlichen Perspektiven.* Marburg: Elwert, 1969. 180 pp.

Law and Jurisprudence

Vollenhoven, Cornelis van. "The Framework of Grotius' Book De Jure Belli ac Pacis (1625). *Verhandelingen der Koninklijke Academie van Wetenschappen te Amsterdam.* Afdeeling Letterkunde. Nieuwe Reeks, Deel 30:4 (1932), 174 pp.

Vrankrijker, A. C. J. de. *De Staatsleer van H. de Groot en zijn Tijdgenoten.* Ph.D. diss., Nijmegen/Utrecht, 1937. 118 pp.

Eysinga, Willem J. M. van. *Gids voor de Groots de Jure Belli ac Pacis.* Leiden: Brill, 1945. 48 pp.

Fortuin, H. *De Natuurrechtelijke Grondslagen van de Groot's Volkenrecht.* The Hague: Martinus Nijhoff, 1946. 254 pp.

Lauterpacht, Hersh. "The Grotian Tradition in International Law." *British Yearbook of International Law* 23 (1946):1–53.

Ottenwälder, Paul. *Zur Naturrechtslehre des Hugo Grotius.* Tübingen: Mohr, 1950. 133 pp.

Oven, J. C. van. "Hugo de Groot's "Inleidinghe" als Lehrbuch des römischen Rechts." *L'Europa e il Diritto Romano . . . in Memoria di P. Koschaker* 1 (1954):269–87.

Welzel, Hans. "Hugo Grotius." In: *Naturrecht und materiale Gerechtigkeit.* 4th ed. Göttingen: Vandenhoeck & Ruprecht, 1962, pp. 123–29.

Wellschmied, Karl. "Zur Inleidinge tot de Hollandsche Rechts-Geleerdheid des Hugo Grotius." *Tijdschrift voor Rechtsgeschiedenis* 20 (1952):389–440.

———. "Zur Entstehung und Bedeutung der Inleidinge tot de Hollandsche Rechts-Geleerdheid von Hugo Grotius." *Zeitschrift für Rechtsgeschichte,* G(ermanistische) A(bteilung) N(eue) F(olge) 69 (1952):155–81.

Pauw, F. de. *Grotius and the Law of the Sea.* Brussels: Editions de l'Institut de Sociologie, 1965. 77 pp.

Wieacker, Franz. "§ 16. Das Zeitalter des Vernunftsrechts." In: *Privatrechtsgeschichte der Neuzeit.* Göttingen: Vandenhoeck & Ruprecht, 1967, pp. 287–301.

Feenstra, Robert. "L'influence de la scholastique espagnole sur Grotius en droit privé." In: *La Seconda Scolastica nella formazione del diritto privato moderno.* Milano: Dott. A. Giuffrè, 1973, pp. 377–402. Reprinted in *Fata Iuris Romani. Etudes d'Histoires du Droit par Robert Feenstra. Leidse Juridische Reeks,* Deel 13. Leiden: University Press, 1974, pp. 338–63.

———. "Hugo de Groot's eerste beschouwingen over *dominium* en over de oorsprong van de private eigendom: *mare liberum* en zijn bronnen." *Acta Juridica. Essays in Honour of Ben Beinert* 1 (1976):269–82.

———. "Der Eigentumsbegriff bei Hugo Grotius im Licht einiger mittelalterlicher und spätscholastischer Quellen." In: *Festschrift für Franz Wieacker zum 70. Geburtstag.* Göttingen: Vandenhoeck & Ruprecht, 1978, pp. 209–34.

Fikentscher, Wolfgang. *De Fide et Perfidia.* Der Treuegedanke in den Staatsparallelen des Hugo Grotius aus heutiger Sicht. Bayerische Akademie der Wissenschaften. Sitzungsberichte 1979, 1. München, 1979. 160 pp.

Selected Bibliography 155

History

Kampinga, Herman. *De Opvattingen over onze Oude Vaderlandsche Geschiedenis bij de Hollandsche Historici der XVIe en XVIIe Eeuw.* Ph.D. diss. Leiden. The Hague: M. Nijhoff, 1917. 207 pp.

Muller, Henri C. A. *Hugo de Groots Annales et Historiae.* Ph.D. diss., University of Utrecht, 1919. 200 pp.

6. Hugo Grotius and Cultural History

Vollenhoven, Cornelis van. "Grotius and Geneva." In: *Bibliotheca Visseriana.* Leiden: Brill, 1926, pp. 1–81.

Lewalter, Ernst. "Die geistesgeschichtliche Stellung des Hugo Grotius." *Deutsche Vierteljahrsschrift für Literaturwissenschaft und Geistesgeschichte* 11 (Stuttgart, 1933):262–93.

Eysinga, W. J. M. van. "Iets over de Groots Jongelingsjaren." *De Gids* 105:4 (1941):36–67.

Voogd, G. J. de. *Erasmus en Grotius.* Leiden: Nederl. Uitgevers, n.d. 198 pp.

Velde, Van de, R. G. "De studie van het Gotisch in de Nederlanden." *Koninklijke Vlaamse Akademie.* Gent, 1966.

Michelis De, Fiorella Pintacuda. *Le Origini Storiche e Culturali del Pensiero di Ugo Grozio.* Publicazioni . . . dell 'Università di Milano. La Nuova Italia Editrice. Florence, 1967. 199 pp.

7. Historical Information Reading List

Important Contemporaries

Johan Van Oldenbarnevelt (1547–1619)

Vries, Theun de. *Oldenbarnevelt.* The Hague: Leopold, 1937; 3rd ed., 1953. 207 pp.

Tex, Jan den. *Oldenbarnevelt.* 1–5. Haarlem: Tjeenk Willink, 1960–1972. 2824 pp. *(sic).* Translated into English, Cambridge University Press, 1973. 759 pp. in 2 vols. Dutch Paperback edition by M. Nijhoff, forthcoming.

Gerlach, H. *Het Proces tegen Oldenbarnevelt en de 'Maximen in den Staet.'* Haarlem: Tjeenk Willink, 1965. 707 pp.

Gerretson, Cornelis. *Moord of Recht? Twee studies over Johan van Oldenbarnevelt.* Baarn: Torenboek, 1969. 102 pp.

Prince Maurits of Nassau (1567–1625)

Hallema, A. *Prins Maurits 1567–1625: Veertig jaren strijder voor's lands vrijheid* [Illustré]. Assen: Barn, 1949. 222 pp.

Daniel Heinsius (1580–1655)

Becker-Cantarino, B. *Daniel Heinsius*. Boston: Twayne Publishers, 1978. 182 pp.

Theologians

Bangs, Carl. *Arminius: A Study in the Dutch Reformation*. Nashville, Tenn./New York: Abingdon Press, 1971. 382 pp.

Itterzon, G. P. van. *Franciscus Gomarus*. The Hague: M. Nijhoff, 1930.

Woude, Cornelis van der. *Sibrandus Lubbertus: Leven en werken*. Proefschrift. Amsterdam: J. H. Kok, 1963. 623 pp.

Patry, Raoul. *Philippe du Plessis-Mornay*. Paris: Fischbacher, 1933. 670 pp.

Rogge, H. C. *Johannes Wtenbogaert en zijn tijd*. 3 vols. Amsterdam: Y. Rogge, 1874–76. 1267 pp.

Teachers/Intellectual Friends/Other Mentors

Oestreich, Gerhard. "Justus Lipsius als Universalgelehrter zwischen Renaissance and Barock." In: *Leiden University in the Seventeenth Century: An Exchange of Learning*. Edited by Th. H. Lunsingh and G. H. M. Posthumus Meyjes. Leiden: University Press/Brill, 1975. 496 pp.; 176–201.

Saunders, Jason Lewis. *Justus Lipsius: The Philosophy of Renaissance Stoicism*. New York: The Liberal Arts Press, 1955. 228 pp.

Bernays, Jacob. *Joseph Justus Scaliger*. Berlin, 1865; rpt. New York: B. Franklin Research & Source Work Series 149, n.d. 319 pp.

Bruehl, C. M. "Josef Justus Scaliger: Ein Beitrag zur geistesgeschichtlichen Bedeutung der Altertumswissenschaft." *Zeitschrift für Religions- und Geistesgeschichte* 12 (1960):201–18; 13 (1961):45–65.

Rademaker, C. S. M. *Life and Work of Gerardus Joannes Vossius (1577–1649)*. van Gorcum: Assen 1981. 462 pp.

8. Intellectual Movements/Summaries

Aken, Lucie J. N. K. van. *De Remonstrantsche Broederschap, verleden en heden*. Arnhem: V. L. Slaterus, 1947. 168 pp.

Berkhof, H. *Geschiedenis der Kerk*. 2d ed. Nijkerk: Callenbach, 1941. 352 pp.

Etter, Else L. *Tacitus in der Geistesgeschichte des 16. und 17. Jahrhunderts*. Basler Beiträge zur Geschichtswissenschaft. 103. Basel, 1966. 225 pp.

Fockema Andreae, S. J. *De Nederlandse Staat onder de Republiek* (offered to the Royal Dutch Academy of Sciences in 1960). Amsterdam: Noord-Holland, 1975. 198 pp.

Gelder, H. A. Enno van. *Getemperde Vrijheid*. Historische Studies 26 (Groningen, 1972). 302 pp.

Heppe, Heinrich. *Reformierte Dogmatik* (= *Die Dogmatik der evangelisch-reformierten Kirche).* Neukirchen, 1935. 579 pp.

Huizinga, Johan. *Dutch Civilization in the Seventeenth Century and Other Essays.* New York: F. Ungar, 1968. Also available in German (1933) and Dutch (1941).

Kaajan, H. *De Groote Synode van Dordrecht in 1618–1619.* Amsterdam: De Standaard, n.d. [1918]. 240 pp.

Lecler, Joseph, S. J. *Histoire de la Tolérance au siècle de la Réforme.* 2 vols. Paris: Montaigne, 1955; in English: London, 1960. Translated into German by Elisabeth Schneider. *Geschichte der Religionsfreiheit im Zeitalter der Reformation.* Stuttgart: Schwabenverlag, 1965. 647 pp. Vol. 2 concerns our period.

Popkin, Richard H. *The History of Scepticism from Erasmus to Descartes.* Wijsgerige Teksten en Studies, 4. Assen: Van Gorcum, 1960. 236 pp.

Price, J. L. *Culture and Society in the Dutch Republic of the 17th Century.* New York: Scribner, 1974.

Wansink, H. *Politieke Wetenschappen aan de Leidse Universiteit 1575– ± 1630.* Ph.D. diss., Utrecht, 1975. 273 pp.

Young, Alexander. *History of the Netherlands (Holland and Belgium).* Boston: Estes & Lauriat, 1884. Still a sweeping introduction for the beginner.

Netherlandic Topography

Guicciardini, L. *Description de Tout le Pays-Bas.* Antwerp, 1567. His own French translation of his Italian original of 1567; first German translation by D. Federmann, 1580; first Latin translation, 1613 and ff.

Index

Anabaptists, 87
Anglican Church, 91
Anti-Socinian, 92
Appetitus societatis, 104
Aratos of Soloi, 30, 47, 126n51
Aristotle, 56, 129n25, 139n48
Arminius: the Cheruscan, 130n42
Arminius, Jacob, 35, 85, 143n114
Asianic style, 79
Athens, New: Leiden, 51
Attic style, 58, 79, 135n65
Aubéry du Maurier, B., 112
Augsburg, Treaty of, 74
Augustus: Roman Emperor, 100, 140n58

Babel, Tower of, 61
Barbeyrac, J., 142n96
Barcley, J., 136n1
Batavia: 17th century Holland, 57, 72–79
Batavian: 17th century Hollander, 65
Belgia: 17th century Netherlands, 77, 79
Belgian: 17th century Netherlander, 66
Bellarmine: Cardinal, 107
Benedict XIV: Pope, 131n50

Béza, Th., 137n14
Bielke, St., 112
Blaeuw, J., 76
Bodin, J., 72
Bor, P., 77
Borren, Alida (Grotius's mother), 1
British-Dutch Truce Conference: The Hague, 1609, 100; The Hague 1615, 99
Bruno, G., 6
Burgundy, Mary of, 71
Bushnell, H., 118, 145n18

Caesar, 67, 79, 135n62
Calovius, A., 63, 132n81
Calvin, J., 137n14, 138n23
Camerarius, J., 63
Camerarius, L., 112
Casaubonus, I., 113, 137n18
Cassiodorus, 83
Catharina, Sta: caravel, 97
Celan, P., 33
Christina: Queen of Sweden, 5, 58, 76, 112
Chrysippos, 139n48
Cicero, 46–48, 79, 104, 133n6, 139n48
Civilis, Julius or Claudius, 57, 71, 130n42

Index

Clausewitz, C. von, 141n88
Cleopatra, 100
Cluverius, Ph., 130n45
Condé, Henri: Prince of France, 124n3
Confessio Belgica, 137n14
Confession, Tridentinian, 94
Coornhert, D. V., 69
Coster, L. J., 133n9
Counter-Remonstrant (Gomarist) faction, 84–90

Dante, 106
Dares: Grotius's nickname, 86, 137n8
Decretum Ordinum, 56
Dordrecht, Synod of, 3, 58, 72, 92

Edward: The Confessor, 82
Edwards, Jonathan, 118
Elizabeth I: Queen of England, 135n58, 140n59
Elzevier, L.: Press 52, 81, 136n69
Empedocles, 60
English East India Company (EEIC), 99
Entellus: Lubbertus's nickname, 86, 137n8, 14, 16
Episcopius, S., 85
Erasmus, 68
Erastes, Th., 136n1
Euripides, 49–50

Ferdinand III: German Emperor, 4
Flavian-Emperors, 76
Frederick Henry: Prince of Orange, 29
Fury, The Spanish: sack of Antwerp, 58

Galileo, 132n84

Gallicanism, 136n1
Gallicanists, 87
Gellius, 139n48
Germanicus, 48
Gheyn, Jacques de, 2, 48
Goethe, J. W., 105
Gomarists: Counter-Remonstrant Faction, 84–90
Gomarus, Fr., 84–85
Graswinckel, Th., 105
Gregory XIV: Pope, 24
Groot, Cornelis de (son), 1
Groot, Diderik de (son), 49
Groot, Franciscus de (brother), 34, 38
Groot, Jan Huigh de (father), 1, 35, 40, 57, 85, 112, 126n49, 144n7
Groot, Pieter de (son), 72, 104, 107, 113, 126n49
Groot, Willem de (brother), 72, 108, 112–14, 125n38, 132n71, 86, 143n114
Gustavus Adolphus: King of Sweden, 107

Hague, Peace Conference of The, 1899: 119; 1907: 119
Hammond, H., 63, 132n80
Hannibal, 32
Heemskerck: Admiral, 135n58
Heinsius, Daniel, 2, 6, 50, 73–75, 81, 112–13, 120–21, 125n41, 134n43
Henry IV: King of France, 2
Hooker, Richard, 90–91, 137n14, 18

Independence, Declaration of, 119
Infralapsarian, 125n30
Isidore, Bishop of Seville, 83

James I: King of England, 28, 84–87, 89, 97, 140n59
Jeanin, P., 135n58
Jordanes, 83, 136n70
Julius (Claudius) Civilis, 57, 71, 130n42
Junius, Fr., 69
Juristenvereeniging, Nederlandsche, of 1912, 120
Jus magistratus, 87
Justinian: Emperor of Byzantium, 127n63, 139n41, 50; *Corpus Juris Civilis*, 94–95; *Codex*, 95–96; *Digests*, 95–96, 105; *Institutions*, 36–37, 61, 95–96, 108

Kallimachos, 52
Köhne, I. von Jasky, 113

Lèse-majesté, 11, 19, 23, 88, 115
Lindenbrog, F., 81
Lingelsheim, G. M., 112–13
Lipsius, J., 53, 56, 58, 77, 87, 111, 133n6, 138n19, 144n1, 3
Livy, 70
Llull, Ramon, 104
Louis XIII: King of France, 4, 80, 115
Lubbertus, Sibrandus, 9, 85–87
Lucanus, M. L., 53–56
Lugo, J. de, 94
Luther, Martin, 63

Margaretha: Lady van Mechelen, 39, 127n73
Marini, C., 112
Martianus Capella, 44, 46, 127n65
Mary: Duchess of Burgundy, 71
Maurits van Nassau, 2, 3, 5, 29–30, 39–40, 48, 56–57, 67, 74, 80, 86–89, 91, 115–17, 125n43

Melanchthon, Ph., 94
Menander, 49
Mennonites, 98
Merula, P., 109, 143n119
Meteren, E. van, 77
Mierevelt, M. J. van, 134n43
Milton, John, 120
Montaigne, Michel de, 53
Münster and Osnabrück, Peace Treaty of, 5, 98, 117

Nazi Trials: Nuremberg, 119

Oldenbarnevelt, Elias (brother), 3
Oldenbarnevelt, Johan van, 2–3, 28, 30–31, 73, 88, 91, 100, 116
Opitz, Martin, 120, 146n29
Ovid, 55
Oxenstierna, Axel, 4, 21, 76, 81, 112, 117

Papinian, 137n11
Paraeus, J. 89
Paul, St., 47
Paulus Diaconus (Warnfried), 81–83
Père Joseph, 4
Philemon, 139n48
Philip II: King of Spain, 27
Philips van Leiden, 145n10
Philo: *Vita Josephi*, 21
Pierce, Th., 63
Planudes, Maximos, 51
Plato, 49, 71, 134n28
Plinius, 46, 82
Plutarch, 33, 49
Prokopius, 81, 136n73, 75
Propertius, 100
Ptolemy, 82
Pufendorf, Samuel, 107, 118–19, 145n19, 20–21

Index

Racine, 58
Raden, Gecommiteerde, 31
Ramus, P., 143n114
Ramistic system, 109
Raphelengius, Chr., 2, 54
Ravesteyn, J. van, 74
Reichsrecht, 95
Reigersbergh, Marie van, de Groot, 3, 15, 31, 52, 112–14, 130n31
Remonstrant (Arminian) faction, 89–90, 93
Reydt, E. van, 77
Rezeptionsgeschichte, 118
Richelieu, Cardinal, 4, 107, 111
Ronsard, P. de, 47

Salvius, J. Adler, 4, 112
Sarravius, Cl., 127n70
Scaliger, J. J., 2, 6, 15, 40, 44, 52, 72
Schmalz, P., 112
Scientia civilis: political science, forerunner of, 67, 133n12
Seneca, 8–9, 12, 54
Selden, John, MP, 99, 140n64
Sidney, Sir Philip, 16
Silius, Titus (Italicus), 125n29
Snellius, R., 126n53
Socinianisterye, 91
Sophocles, 49–50
Spinola, A. de, 107
Stevin, Simon, 40, 67, 69, 126n53, 128n77–78, 133n21
Stobaeus, J., 49–50, 139n48
Stoic-Attic (*stoattic) style, 80
Suárez, Fr., 141n89
Supralapsarian, 137n14
Synod: of Dordrecht, 3, 58, 72, 92

Tacitus, 56, 58, 67, 71, 76, 78–79, 135n51, 64

Thales, 61
Thuanus, Franciscus, (De Thou, François) (son), 31, 38
Thuanus, J. A., 73, 126n56

Uitenbogaert, J., 2, 84–86, 136n2
Ulfila: Bishop, 81
Ulpian, 139n48
Uniformity, Act of, 89
Urban VIII: Pope, 64
Utrecht, Union of, 74

Vaenius, O., 57
Valdés, Fr. de, 32
Varro Grammaticus, 46
Velasques, Diego, 106
Velde, W. C. v. d., 108
Vico, G., 120, 146n31
Virgil, 46, 54–55, 86, 100, 137n8, 10
VOC (United Dutch East Indies Company), 2, 27, 97–99, 100–102
Vondel, Joost v. d., 31, 120, 124n15
Vorstius, C., 84–87, 91, 137n4
Vossius, G. J., 15, 21, 36, 38, 72, 76, 112–13, 125n36, 127n64, 145n15
Vossius, Isaac (son) 81
Vulcanius, Bonaventura, 44

Werff, Pieter v. d., 32
Wheaton, Henry, 119
White, W., 63
Wilson, Woodrow, 119
Wise, John, 118–19, 145n20, 22
Willem, Prince of Orange ("The Silent"), 29, 32

Xenophon, 49

DATE DUE

NOV 12 1993